CULTURES OF THE WORLD®

MADAGASCAR

Jay Heale & Zawiah Abdul Latif

Marshall Cavendish
Benchmark

New York

PICTURE CREDITS
Cover photo: © Pete Oxford/Danita Delimont Stock Photography
Alamy: 48 • alt.TYPE / Reuters: 12, 28, 36, 92 • Bjorn Klingwall: 3, 9, 34, 43, 44, 71, 83, 84, 95, 125 • Corbis Inc.: 39 • Focus Team Italy: 7, 14, 16, 17, 21, 66, 70, 90, 101, 109, 119, 127 • Francis Tan: 130, 131 • Getty Images: 30, 35, 40, 41, 47, 54, 59, 68, 112, 114 • H. Brad / C.O.P.: 20, 72, 79, 91, 99, 116, 117 • Hulton Getty: 26, 27 • Hutchison Library: 11, 49, 62, 77, 81, 86, 87, 88, 105, 106, 110, 122 • Jay Heale: 32, 97, 123 • Lonely Planet Images: 1, 6, 19, 50, 51, 53, 58, 61, 63, 64, 75, 78, 82, 94, 100, 128 • National Geographic Image Collection: 4, 5, 22, 38, 56, 57, 76, 108, 113, 118, 121 • North Wind Pictures: 24, 103 • Photolibrary. com: 15, 60, 69, 73, 124 • Ron Emmons: 18 • Pietro Scozzari: 93, 111 • Still Pictures: 23, 46, 67 • TopFoto: 31

PRECEDING PAGE
A group of smiling village children.

Publisher (U.S.): Michelle Bisson
Editors: Deborah Grahame, Mabelle Yeo, Mindy Pang
Copyreader: Daphne Hougham
Designer: Geoslyn Lim
Cover picture researcher: Connie Gardner
Picture researcher: Thomas Khoo

Marshall Cavendish Benchmark
99 White Plains Road
Tarrytown, NY 10591
Web site: www.marshallcavendish.us

© Times Media Private Limited 1998
© Marshall Cavendish International (Asia) Private Limited 2009
® "Cultures of the World" is a registered trademark of Times Publishing Limited.

Originated and designed by Times Media Private Limited
An imprint of Marshall Cavendish International (Asia) Private Limited
A member of Times Publishing Limited

Marshall Cavendish is a trademark of Times Publishing Limited.

All Internet sites were correct and accurate at the time of printing. All monetary figures in this publication are in U.S. dollars.

Library of Congress Cataloging-in-Publication Data

Heale, Jay.
   Madagascar / by Jay Heale & Zawiah Abdul Latif. — 2nd ed.
     p. cm. — (Cultures of the world)
   Summary: "Provides comprehensive information on the geography, history,
     wildlife, governmental structure, economy, cultural diversity, peoples,
     religion, and culture of Madagascar"—Provided by publisher.
   Includes bibliographical references and index.
   ISBN 978-0-7614-3036-0
   1. Madagascar—Juvenile literature. I. Latif, Zawiah Abdul. II. Title.

DT469.M28H43 2008
969.1—dc22   2007048288

Printed in China
7 6 5 4 3 2 1

CONTENTS

Life is simple in the villages, and it is common to see people carrying goods slung at one or both ends of a pole supported on a shoulder.

These prickly *didierea*, the octopus tree, are unique to Madagascar. Despite their spiny appearance, they are not cacti but trees.

INTRODUCTION

MADAGASCAR HAS BEEN CALLED "the island at the end of the earth" by a Malagasy poet because, beyond its southern tip, there is only open sea all the way to the Antarctic. This geographical isolation has bestowed a staggering profusion of flora and fauna upon Madagascar that is found nowhere else in the world.

A rich mix of people makes up Madagascar. Early settlers came from various regions in Southeast Asia, Polynesia, India, Arabia, and East Africa. Such diversity in cultures is especially evident in the use of the Malagasy language, with its many regional variations. The Malagasy, however, are united in the complex system of beliefs that they attach to every aspect of living and dying. It is this very solidarity that has enabled them to survive foreign interventions, political upheavals, and social and economic adversity. Although the country is relatively successful in foreign trade and industry, subsistence farming remains the mainstay of the economy. Poverty is rife, and Madagascar's economic survival is heavily dependent on foreign aid and the preservation of its delicate natural environment.

GEOGRAPHY

MOST PEOPLE KNOW OF MADAGASCAR as a large island situated off the southeastern coast of Africa. In the process of continental drift, the massive chunk broke away from the mainland of Africa about 165 million years ago and has been cut off ever since, which explains why more than 80 percent of its plants and animals are exclusive to the island. The mainland now lies some 250 miles (400 km) to the west, across the Mozambique Channel.

Madagascar is the fourth-largest island in the world, after Greenland, New Guinea, and Borneo. It has a landmass of 226,657 square miles (587,040 square km), including its offshore islands. One thousand miles (1,609 km) long, Madagascar is approximately twice the size of the state of Arizona and has about three times as many people. There are no particularly high mountains, but a high plateau, ranging in height from 2,450 to 4,430 feet (750 to 1,350 m), runs down its north-south axis like a backbone.

Four-fifths of the population of about 19.4 million live on what they can produce from the land. When there is not enough land for growing rice or grazing cattle, trees in the remaining forest are cut down and the timber used as fuel. This is an ecological disaster, especially when considering that the dwindling forests are the homes of unique creatures found nowhere else in the world. The exposed earth is then subjected to erosion, and the nutrient-rich topsoil capable of supporting better crops is washed away into the ocean.

Above: **Madagascar is home to about a quarter of the world's plant and animal kingdoms.**

Opposite: **A beautiful view of Madagascar's hilly terrain near Diégo-Suarez in Antsiroñana in the extreme north.**

7

Rice, a Madagascan staple food, being planted in the highlands. The demand for farmland has cost the nation whole forests, cut and burned to make way for rice—and erosion.

Politically, the island is divided into 22 regions, including Anamalanga in the central highlands, Sofia to the northwest, Sava to the northeast, Diana on the northern tip, Atsimo-Andrefana on the southwest, and Vatovavy-Fitovinany on the southeast.

CENTRAL HIGHLANDS

The high plateau forming the spine of Madagascar is the land of the Merina, the most numerous, and once most powerful, of the Malagasy clans. It is still the most prosperous area in the country. Rolling hills form pastures for the humpback zebu cattle, while the valleys are terraced with rice fields. In the west, the hills turn bare and dry; in the east, forested slopes lead to the narrow coastal plain. At Périnet Reserve, reached by road from Antananarivo, there is a population of indri, the largest of the lemur species. Semiprecious stones such as jasper, rose quartz, sapphire, tourmaline, and amethyst are found in small quantities in the mountains. Snow is not uncommon on the highlands in the winter.

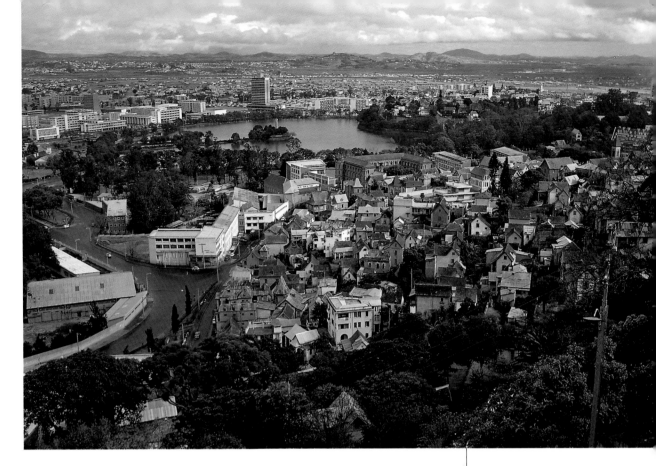

ANTANANARIVO

Surrounded by the twelve sacred hills of the Imerina plateau is Antananarivo (usually shortened to Tana), the capital of Madagascar. Meaning "city of the thousand" in Malagasy, it is a growing city of more than 1.7 million people. Not only is it Madagascar's largest city, it is also its administrative, communications, and economic center. The city sprawls over a curving ridge, with a central square that once housed the world-famous market Zoma on one side and Lake Anosy and a World War I memorial on the other.

The road system is so complex that, as one resident put it, "a compass would get confused, let alone a visitor." The long and straight Avenue de l'Indépendence runs through the poorer and lower area, changes its name to Avenue du 26 Juin as it passes through the relocated market area, and then plunges through a tunnel under the Upper Town to merge with L. Jean Ralaimongo Road beside the lake. There, drivers can turn left to the soccer stadium or right to the Hilton Hotel, one of the few high-rise buildings in town.

The development of Antananarivo began under the French colonial administration during the late 19th and early 20th centuries.

In the Upper Town lies the Presidential Palace, with government buildings clustered around it. Some of the better hotels, like the Colbert Hotel and the Radama Hotel, are in this area, as also is the tourist office that distributes free maps and advice.

Higher, in the skyline, are the four towers of the Queen's Palace and the associated Royal Village, known as the Rova. Both the palace and the village were gutted by fire in November 1995, and all that remains are rows of arched windows gaping at the sky. Fortunately, many of the historic items that had been on display were saved from the fire. Although restoration of the palace has begun, limited funding has made the progress rather slow. On this higher ridge also stand several Catholic churches, four of them dedicated to Malagasy martyrs, and many schools.

THE SOUTH

The southern areas are a mixture of semidesert, coral-fringed beaches, nature reserves, scrub-covered hills, and the stark sandstone peaks of L'Isalo National Park. This is the driest part of Madagascar—a "spiny" desert where baobab, aloe, and spiky green octopus trees (similar to but unrelated to cactus) live in a tangle of thorny scrub. Large areas have been cleared to grow sisal, processed for cordage, which stand in pointy green rows in the red soil. The French introduced the prickly pear cactus from Mexico, and it is used as natural fencing and for feeding cattle.

Only 5 miles (8 km) east of this semidesert, separated by a mountain range, is a tropical east coast jungle and the breezy town of Tôlanaro. It is also known as Fort Dauphin, taking its name from the French-built fort there that now lies in ruins. Residents of the town prefer its Malagasy name, but most guidebooks retain the French colonial name. The town is built on a peninsula with a small harbor on one side, overlooked by the red-painted Palais de Justice. A large crucifix stands on a hill above the town. Hotels and restaurants in the area cater to the needs of tourists.

Fragments of fossilized eggs belonging to the extinct "elephant bird," a giant flightless bird native to Madagascar, have been found in this region. Two popular nature reserves are the Berenty and Kaleta parks, which serve as a refuge for ringtail and brown lemurs, as well as the creamy-white sifaka lemurs and huge fruit bats. The tamarind gallery forest is found among the lush green undergrowth of the eastern coastal strip, also home to the rare three-cornered palm and the carnivorous pitcher plant.

Tôlañaro in southeastern Madagascar, facing the Indian Ocean, is also called Fort Dauphin, after the French East India Company fort of the same name.

A desolate view of the district of Ambanja, where numerous houses were destroyed by a cyclone.

THE EAST

The eastern part of Madagascar, with its almost straight coastline, is known as the Whale Highway because of the migrating humpback whales that gather offshore to breed. It is also nicknamed the Pirate Coast because of legends about the presence of pirates in the area in the past. An inland waterway, the Pangalanes Canal, runs parallel to the shore. This is a 375-mile (603-km) chain of lakes and canals that was once thronged with canoes carrying great loads of fruit and vegetables. Now clogged with reeds and water hyacinths, it is used mainly for local fishing.

The eastern shoreline is a fertile area drenched with tropical rains from December to March. It is also known as the Cyclone Coast, after the hurricanes that originate in the tropics. In 2007 Madagascar was hit by six tropical cyclones in what was one of the country's worst cyclone seasons. Historically, the most destructive cyclones include the one that severely damaged the city of Toamasina in 1927, and a storm that tore across the offshore island of Nosy Boraha (nosy means "island" in Malagasy), also called Sainte Marie, in 1986. Another was Cyclone Geralda, which struck the same area in February 1994, wrecking roads and railways and leaving 500,000 people homeless. The worst cyclones to hit Madagascar in the past twenty years were Gafilob and Elita, which struck the country twice in ten days in February 2004, leaving 309,500 people affected by its devastation. Schools and health centers were either damaged or destroyed, and 74 people were killed. The government estimated that the total economic toll of the cyclone was more than $250 million. These hurricanes, combined with centuries of slash-and-burn clearing of rain forests, have eroded the steep slopes of Madagascar's terrain, causing gaping red holes in the landscape known as *lavaka* (LA-vak).

Toamasina on the east coast is Madagascar's largest port, exporting sugar, coffee, cloves, and rice. It is connected to the capital by road, rail, and air. The town has a population of over 206,000 and is a popular holiday resort for residents. Nosy Boraha, farther north, boasts the world's only pirate graveyard. As it is unlikely that any of the most infamous pirates of Madagascar are buried there, it perhaps does not matter that wind and rain have erased most of the carved inscriptions. The country's largest lake, Alaotra, was once in a wooded area. Then, as has happened throughout much of Madagascar, the trees were cut down to provide land for the cultivation of crops and grazing for cattle. The soil eroded and washed into the lake, which is now less than a third of its original size. The town of Ambatondrazaka once fronted the lake but is now 4.35 miles (7 km) from the water.

High rainfall makes this the greenest part of the island. Cloves, vanilla, coffee, and fruit are grown for export, and rare orchids flourish. The ocean shoreline is picturesque, although swimmers have to be wary of sharks. Sometimes gold cups and coins are found washed up on the beach, fueling hopeful tales of buried pirate treasure.

"Madagascar is truly the naturalist's promised land. Here nature seems to have withdrawn into a private sanctuary in order to work on designs which are different from those she has created elsewhere."

—*Joseph Philibert Commerson, a visitor to the island in 1770.*

THE NORTH

Much of northern Madagascar is cut off by the rugged Tsarataňana massif (mountain mass), which is the locale of extinct volcanic mountains, as well as the island's highest peak of 9,436 feet (2,876 m), Maromokotro. Differing altitudes of these mountains cause varied weather conditions, ranging from sporadic heavy rains to dry and cool periods.

The area around Antsiraňana on the east is dry, while the island-strewn coastline around Nosy Be in the west has higher rainfall. Antsiraňana, which is also known as Diégo-Suarez, has one of the finest deepwater harbors in the world. During its history, the port has accommodated slavers, pirates, a French naval base built in 1885, and the British during World War II. A legend tells of the existence of a 17th-century republic, Libertalia, founded there by pirates.

Local industries include shipbuilding, tuna fishing, salt extraction, and agriculture. Inland, there is Amber Mountain National Park, a volcanic massif covered with forest. Picturesque waterfalls with malachite kingfishers and varieties of bats attract tourists, while the dense trees conceal chameleons, orchids, and endangered species of lemur. Crocodiles live in the humid underground caves, and there are several species of shrimps, according to studies initiated by the World Wildlife Fund (WWF).

Farther south is Ankarana, an area of weirdly shaped, razor-sharp limestone pinnacles known as *tsingy* (TSING-i), meaning spikes. Local communities, who have buried several of their kings in one of the caves there, consider the area sacred.

The island of Nosy Be was one of the two early French footholds near the mainland. The other was the island of Nosy Boraha, also known as Sainte Marie. Both are valuable tourist destinations on the Indian Ocean.

14

Nosy Be, meaning "big island," is a popular tourist destination. The increasing numbers of tourists pronounce this "NOSS-i BAY," but residents prefer "noosh BAY." Its setting of fertile greenery, vanilla plantations, and sweet-smelling yellow ylang-ylang blossoms, which are used to make perfume—combined with fine beaches and stunning marine life for those keen on snorkeling—make for a perfect holiday. There are expensive hotels catering to wealthy visitors and also low-priced ones for the budget conscious. The moneymaking atmosphere here, however, is not representative of Madagascar as a whole.

The main town on Nosy Be is Hell-Ville, named after Admiral de Hell (a former governor of the neighboring island of Réunion), but most visitors stay in beach-hotel complexes. Excursions take tourists to Lokobe, a fragment of preserved forest, or to the highest point on the island, Mont Passot, which has deep blue crater lakes. The smaller islands can be reached by boat. An amazing variety of coral, starfish, anemones, turtles, and fish can be found in the clear waters, and diving tours are available. The nearby island of Nosy Komba is an unofficial sanctuary for black lemurs.

Very fragrant ylang-ylang blossoms, found growing in Nosy Be, are commonly used as a perfume base.

THE WEST

The western slopes of Madagascar were once thickly forested; today only clumps of deciduous trees on dry, open savanna grassland remain. From the air, the land looks crinkled, with long looping rivers that split and join again. The Sakalava people live here; their kingdom, which once

Fishing along the west coast supplements the traditional diet staples of rice and cassava.

dominated the entire region, was the most powerful in Malagasy history. The two main towns are Mahajanga and Morondava, although the areas are now sparsely populated and, in some rocky districts, uninhabited. The coast has mangrove swamps, sweeping sandy beaches, and coral reefs. The endangered Madagascar fish eagle, one of the world's rarest raptors, can sometimes be seen.

Mahajanga, at the mouth of the Betsiboka River, is the second-largest port on the island, and it is strategically positioned for trade with Africa and the Middle East. Founded probably by Arabs, Mahajanga was once a major supply depot for slave traders. It is a hot, busy, windblown town with a mixed population and a strong business community, much of which is Indian. A number of churches and mosques can be found throughout the area.

Local industries include meat, vegetable oil processing, and the cultivation and export of coffee and sugar. At the end of summer, people customarily burn the coarse old grass to generate fresh new growth for the cattle in spring. Unfortunately, when the grass is burned off, nothing remains to stop the topsoil from washing off the fields in heavy rainfall. The sea that lies off the coast of Mahajanga is stained bloodred by silt from the Betsiboka River. Some Mahajangans own holiday cottages on the beach at Amborovy, near an area of strangely eroded red and mauve rock shapes known as Cirque Rouge.

Much farther south lies Morondava. Once grand with seaside villas, it suffers from encroaching sand and increasing poverty. The sea claims at least 3 feet (0.9 m) every year in spite of concrete breakwaters and rocks held together with wire nets to protect the shoreline. Fishermen venture out in dugout canoes trailing nets, coconut palms bend against the wind, and inland, children tend herds of zebu cattle among baobab trees with huge trunks. It has a soccer stadium, dance clubs, and several restaurants serving fresh seafood. Although rain falls there during only four months of the year, there are areas of intense farming cultivation where huge cleared circles are irrigated with rotating water systems.

Bemaraha Tsingy, Madagascar's largest nature reserve at 375,600 acres (152,000 ha), lies between Mahajanga and Morondava and has an almost inaccessible maze of limestone needles and canyons as well as remote tombs of the Vazimba people, reputedly the country's earliest inhabitants. Toliara, in the southwest, is a fishing port and sisal-processing center. Crops such as peanuts, rice, and cotton are grown there.

A major product of the southern region is sisal, used to make sacking, rope, and matting.

CLIMATE

Madagascar's climate is mostly tropical. The prevailing trade winds bring rain from the southeast, while monsoon winds blow from the northwest, resulting in more rain in the north than in the south. Rainfall varies from torrential storms on the east coast during February and March to dry conditions on the southwest, which may receive only 14 inches (36 cm) of rain a year. In general, the summer months from November to April are the wettest, with northwest air currents bringing the rain.

BAOBAB TREES

The baobab is sometimes described as an "upside-down tree" because it looks as if someone had plucked it from the earth and shoved it back in with its roots in the air. In fact, it may be wrong to classify it as a tree at all because it is a succulent plant that stores water in its trunk. Unlike most trees, it does not die when the bark is stripped off. The bark is used to make fibrous cloth, baskets, strings for musical instruments, and waterproof hats. The lightweight wood is used for fishing floats and canoes. The leaves are eaten like spinach, the seeds provide oil, the empty seed husks are used as utensils, and the pulp makes a refreshing drink.

There are eight species of baobab in the world: six are found only in Madagascar, and the others in Africa and Australia. They can live for several thousand years, so many of the baobabs on Madagascar were alive long before man arrived on the island. An impressive avenue of giant baobabs stands near Morondava, and tourists are often taken there to view two baobabs entwined like lovers.

Average summer temperatures range from 77°F (25°C) around the capital to 84°F (29°C) on the coast. Temperatures on the central highlands can drop to freezing during winter nights from June to August.

FLORA AND FAUNA

Madagascar's unique plants and animals are major tourist attractions. Approximately 12,000 plants have been identified, representing about a third of the plants found in Africa. Madagascar not only has a record number of species unique to the island, but because of the continuing loss of forest cover, it also has one of the most threatened ecosystems in the world, plus more endangered species than any other country in Africa. For the Malagasy, rice cultivation and cattle raising are two of their most vital economic activities, and these cannot be carried out in a forest. As a result, trees have been cut down steadily for hundreds of years, so only about 20 percent of the original forests remain. It is estimated that Madagascar lost about 30 million acres (12 million ha) of forest between 1960 and 2000.

There are now 60 protected areas (nature reserves and national parks) maintained in partnership with the World Wildlife Fund, and traditional healers work with a team of Malagasy students to catalog the wealth of medicinal plants in the northern forests. The rosy periwinkle, for example,

The brightly colored flower of the pitcher plant attracts and traps insects in search of nectar. The plant's enzymes break down the proteins of trapped insects into a form it can absorb as nutrient.

Madagascar has many types of chameleons, lizards that can change the color of their skin to blend in with their natural surroundings—ideal as camouflage.

provides an essential compound used to treat childhood leukemia. Overseas agencies, such as the United States Agency for International Development and the United Nations Educational, Scientific and Cultural Organization (UNESCO), also help to fund ecological preservation.

Among Madagascar's most famous mammals are the lemurs, which have apparently undergone little evolutionary change since the Eocene period about 50 million years ago. Another unusual animal is the tenrec, which looks like a tiny hedgehog with yellow and black stripes and bristling spines that rattle when it is angry. Among the 33 species of tenrec, some are furry. The largest is the size of a rabbit and is considered a food delicacy. There are 37 species of bats, including fruit bats that are also known as flying foxes. Among the mongooselike carnivores is the fossa, which can be as large and as vicious as a puma. A rabbit-size, giant jumping rat, not unlike a wallaby, also lives there.

TREES FOR LIFE

The Madagascar Program of the WWF published the following quote by Chief Bakary from the village of Ajavimihavanana in northern Madagascar, as he shared with his people a new appreciation of tree conservation: "Last night, our ancestors spoke to me in a vision. They revealed that God gave us four important trees for life. He gave us the mango tree for its sweet fruit and plentiful shade. He gave us the kapok (silk cotton), tree because we can use the fruit fibers to weave mats to rest and meditate on. He gave us the avocado tree so that we can sell its fruit and make a profit. And finally, God gave us the jackfruit tree as a symbol of friendship. By knocking on the fruit, we can tell if it is ripe by the sound it makes. Therefore the jackfruit is our friend because it can communicate with us."

LEMURS

The ancestors of the lemurs on Madagascar may have drifted from the African mainland on logs. Without any large predators on the island, they evolved freely, and today there are varieties ranging from the mouse lemurs to giant, bearlike lemurs. Some species became extinct after man arrived on the island. The remaining 60 species and subspecies are constantly threatened by the slash-and-burn clearing of the forests.

Lemurs are not monkeys, although they are the closest living descendants of the common ancestor of the monkeys. Other survivors of this line are the bush babies of Africa. Monkeys are more clever than lemurs, which are more primitive and gentle primates. Lemurs live largely on fruit and insects. Their long noses give them a highly developed sense of smell. About half the 33 species are nocturnal, including the strangest of all, the aye-aye.

The aye-aye looks like a large-headed squirrel with bat's ears, a fox's tail, and tiny hands with a bony middle finger that it uses to dig for grubs or pick out the kernels from nuts.

Unfortunately, many superstitious Malagasy believe that the aye-aye bring bad luck. They fear that the "crooked finger" may point out the next person to die, so many aye-aye have been deliberately killed. Aye-aye have also incurred the anger of farmers because they have a sweet tooth and raid coconuts and sugarcane. There is a protected aye-aye reserve on the island of Nosy Mangabe.

In the reptile world, Madagascar claims to be home to half of the world's species of chameleons. A chameleon's eyes swivel independently, allowing it to look forward and backward at the same time. A Malagasy proverb advises, "Be like the chameleon—keep one eye on the past and one eye on the future." There are also fringed geckos, boa constrictors, several species of tortoises and marine turtles, and over 300 butterflies and moths. Birds are harder to spot. Among the rarer birds is the Madagascar flufftail.

Madagascar is considered one of the richest floral kingdoms in the world, with estimates of the number of species exceeding 12,000. There are, for example, 170 species of palms and 1,000 species of orchids. Many of the orchids grow on trees, where they live in harmony (not as parasites) with the tree, collecting water as it runs down the trunk.

HISTORY

ALTHOUGH THE EARLY history of Madagascar is somewhat foggy, it is thought that human beings first set foot on the shores of the island shortly after the birth of Jesus Christ.

Madagascar apparently was uninhabited until about 2,000 years ago when the earliest settlers arrived—not from Africa in the west as one might have guessed, but from the Malay Peninsula and Indonesia, 4,000 miles (6,436 km) to the east. Some think that they might have sailed straight across the Indian Ocean to Madagascar. Others believe the process took longer, with explorers making their way southwest through India, Arabia, and Africa, intermarrying with local groups and acquiring their ethnic mix along the way. Known more in local legend than in fact, these earliest inhabitants were called the Vazimba and were considered the ancestral guardians of the land. Beginning in the seventh century, when Sumatra controlled trade in the Indian Ocean, more settlers, including Muslim traders, arrived. Different ethnic groups began to stake out various areas of the island to control as their own.

Above: **Fishermen rigging a pirogue at Bombetoka Bay in Madagascar.**

Opposite: **Merina tribal ruins near Antananarivo, which were caused by the18th-century warfare.**

EUROPEAN ARRIVALS

In 1500 Portuguese sailors were the first Europeans to arrive. They named their discovery the Isle of Saint Lawrence, but did not stay any longer than did later arrivals, the Dutch and the English. None of them thought the island was worth colonizing. The French did establish a colony in 1642, but plagued with disease and constant attacks by the local inhabitants, they packed up and left. More permanent residents were the bands of pirates operating in the area, especially along the eastern shore, washed by the immense Indian Ocean.

PIRATES

When the rich hauls of the West Indies pirates began to dwindle, the buccaneers of the sea diverted their attention to the trade routes around the Cape of Good Hope, India, and the East Indies. The east coast of Madagascar was an ideal base, and Nosy Boraha became their "home port." The island is a thin strip of land with coconut-fringed beaches surrounded by shallow seas. Captain William Kidd, an English buccaneer, arrived aboard his first ship, the *Adventure*, in 1695, starting a life of piracy that ended on the gallows in London. Other infamous names include another English pirate, John Avery, American pirate Thomas Tew, and Frenchman Olivier Levasseur, also known as La Buse, meaning "The Buzzard," or possibly "The Fool." The names on the tombstones in the pirate graveyard in Nosy Boraha have long since worn away, but one skull and crossbones emblem can still be seen.

In the west, the Menabe peoples, with the help of firearms bought from European traders, extended their rule into the highlands as far as Bengy on the Sakalava River. Sakalava became the name of the people in that region. King Andriamisara I of the Menabe and his successor, Andriandahifotsy, came close to uniting southern and eastern Madagascar. Their successors ruled until the early 19th century, nearly 200 years.

Robert Drury, a British sailor shipwrecked on Madagascar in 1703, stayed for 16 years as a slave, royal butcher, and refugee. His journal is regarded as a historical source, although some commentators suspect that it was actually ghostwritten by Daniel Defoe, who padded Drury's story with descriptions written in 1658 by Etienne de Flacourt (a French governor of Madagascar) and added some reflections of his own. Defoe is the well-known author of the story of Robinson Crusoe.

On the east coast, the pirate hotbed on Nosy Boraha attracted buccaneers from far away, and a 40-gun fort was built there to protect pirated goods. Around 1716, Ratsimilaho, the son of an English pirate and a Malagasy princess, united many of the rival coastal clans into the empire of Betsimisaraka, which means "those who stand together."

In 1750 his daughter Bety married a shipwrecked French corporal, and Ratsimilaho gave them the island of Nosy Boraha as a wedding gift.

Upon Ratsimilaho's death, Princess Bety ruled in her father's place and ceded the island to France. Her son, who ruled after her, was unable to control local uprisings, and the Betsimisaraka kingdom shrank, becoming a single port.

THE MERINA KINGDOMS

In the meantime, the Merina people, led by King Andrianampoinimerina and his successor, Radama, were steadily increasing their domination of the central highlands by using weapons gained through trade agreements with European powers. In 1810 King Radama I modernized the army and, with 35,000 men, established the largest kingdom yet in Madagascar. Unable to defeat the Sakalava kingdom of Menabe, Radama I arranged a marriage between his daughter and the Menabe king Ramitraho. Radama established positive relations with European powers, as well. A Frenchman was the general of his army and an Englishman, his adviser.

The capital was moved to Antananarivo by 1800, and the lucrative slave trade was stopped. In 1820 Britain signed a treaty recognizing Madagascar as an independent state under Merina rule. The London Missionary Society sent missionaries and converted the Merina court to Christianity. The missionaries taught skills to the people so that they could become blacksmiths, carpenters, printers, or weavers. The British also devised a Latin alphabet for the Merina dialect of Malagasy and set up a printing press. As a result, Merina culture began to spread over Madagascar.

In the late 1830s, King Radama's widow and successor, Queen Ranavalona I, declared Christianity illegal and killed many converts. Four churches in the capital city now stand in memory of those early martyrs. Her son, Radama II, ascended the throne in 1861 and established religious freedom. He improved the judicial system and encouraged foreign trade. Christianity became more or less official in Madagascar. Radama II was assassinated, however, after only two years on the throne.

"The greatest single pirate stronghold the world has ever known."

—*T. V. Bulpin, writing about Madagascar in his book* Islands in a Forgotten Sea

A FRENCH COLONY

Competing European powers played a key role in the next chapter of Madagascar's history. In 1890 France and Britain signed a treaty in which French control over Madagascar was recognized in return for British sovereignty in Zanzibar. The French selected Mahajanga as the base for their expeditionary force, which marched into Antananarivo. By the time they arrived in the capital on September 30, 1895, the invading French force had shrunk to 4,000 men—over 11,000 had died of disease along the way. But since sickness and starvation had also struck and weakened the Merina forces, the French still managed to capture the capital. In 1896 they set up a colonial administration with Joseph Galliéni as governor-general. In 1897 the French exiled the reigning Merina queen and turned Madagascar into a French protectorate.

Galliéni proclaimed French the official language and tried to suppress both the Malagasy language and the earlier British influence. The colonial settlers cleared the forests to make way for sugarcane, cotton, and coffee plantations. Harsh taxation resulted in forced labor for those unable to pay, and many peasants were compelled to work in conditions of semislavery. Although the island was developed under French rule, and there were construction projects and visible economic progress, among the people there were increasing resentments and an accelerating desire for national independence.

During the early stages of World War II, France fell to Germany. This resulted in the British forces' occupying several major towns, including Antananarivo and the port of Diégo-Suarez, to prevent the harbor from falling into Japanese hands, as they were allies of Germany. Madagascar was handed back to the French, led by General Charles de Gaulle, in 1943, and became an Overseas Territory of France (an administrative division of France outside of Europe) in 1946. In the highland plateau, though, the smoldering struggle for political rights by the Merina led to

During King Radama II's reign, French Roman Catholics and English Protestants vied for power, resulting in a revolt against the king's European-influenced policies.

an uprising in March 1947 that was crushed ruthlessly by the French army. Several thousand Malagasy were killed, and the leaders were either executed or exiled. Seeing the way that the political winds were blowing, however, the French then began to let go and to transfer political power to the leaders of the coastal regions.

In 1958 the Malagasy people voted in a referendum to become an autonomous republic within the French community of overseas nations. Independence was at last achieved on June 26, 1960 (now celebrated as Independence Day), and Philibert Tsiranana was elected as the first president of the Malagasy Republic.

THE FIRST REPUBLIC

The recent history of Madagascar has been greatly influenced by the struggles for power between two main ethnic groups: the *côtiers* (COH-ti-ay), or coastal people, and the highland Merina. Although supposedly independent, Madagascar continued to be dominated by France, which remained in control of trade and financial institutions. President Tsiranana was pro-French and refused to establish diplomatic relations with Communist countries. The Merina disliked him because he was a *côtier*. The economy fell into a slump, and uprisings were suppressed as harshly as they had been under French rule.

Massive antigovernment demonstrations took place in 1972, forcing President Tsiranana to resign. The civilian government was replaced by a military one when General Gabriel Ramanantsoa was appointed prime minister. A period of martial law followed during which a new leader, Colonel Richard Ratsimandrava, was shot dead within a week of taking office. In June 1975 the Supreme Council of the Revolution, led by Admiral Didier Ratsiraka, ushered in a Christian-Marxist one-party state, changing the name of the country from the Malagasy Republic to the Democratic Republic of Madagascar.

After England agreed, the French legislature passed a law making Madagascar a French colony. General Joseph Galliéni was sent to subdue the Merina and abolish its monarchy.

Didier Ratsiraka wielded power over three terms as president (from 1975 to 1992) before being deposed. He was later reelected in 1997 but lost in the 2001 elections.

THE SECOND REPUBLIC

President Ratsiraka found himself at the helm of a country with a shattered economy and a nonexistent educational system. Banks, insurance companies, and major businesses were nationalized. Ties with France were cut, and military help was welcomed from the Soviet Union. A debt crisis in 1981, however, forced Ratsiraka to rethink these reforms and return to a free market economy in 1986. In 1982 he was reelected to a second seven-year term, but mounting unrest forced him to allow opposition parties to be introduced during the run-up to the 1989 elections. In spite of this, he was elected to a third term as president. Widespread allegations of ballot rigging abounded, and a string of protest riots erupted. Amid the fall of Communism in Eastern Europe and the crumbling of the Soviet Union, Ratsiraka maintained friendly relations with North Korea and made trade agreements with the apartheid government of South Africa.

The main opposition, the Forces Vives, called for general strikes. Nearly half a million people staged demonstrations in front of the presidential palace, demanding democracy. The presidential guard opened fire on the demonstrators and many were killed. In November 1991 President Ratsiraka relinquished power, but refused to step down from his official position.

A transitional government was formed to draft a new constitution that was approved by referendum in August 1992. This declared Madagascar to be a unitary state with multiparty democracy and reduced the executive powers of the president. In the subsequent presidential elections, Professor Albert Zafy, a French-trained professor of surgery and leader of the Forces Vives, was elected, ending 17 years of Ratsiraka's virtual dictatorship. Zafy became the first president of the Third Republic in March 1993.

THE THIRD REPUBLIC

The Third Republic was not immune to problems. President Zafy was soon impeached, in 1996, for corruption and unconstitutional exercise of power. Zafy's government was also ineffective in implementing IMF-led (International Monetary Fund) policies to modernize and promote Madagascar's economy. The increasingly distressed population held public demonstrations and called for a military government in response to the worsening economic situation. In the ensuing presidential elections of 1997, former president Ratsiraka emerged the winner. A 1998 referendum returned more power to the presidency, making impeachment more difficult and allowing the president to dissolve parliament.

The next round of presidential elections in 2001 led to political disaster when Ratsiraka's main opponent, Marc Ravalomanana, contested the electoral results on the grounds that Ratsiraka had rigged the election. A six-month political crisis ensued, and Madagascar's economy virtually came to a standstill as violence broke out among rival protesters. The charismatic Ravalomanana was eventually declared president in May 2002. He began implementing economic reforms that won the support of donors and investors from the West. Although poverty remained endemic, Ravalomanana did manage to return the economy to preconflict levels and to retire foreign debt.

Before the 2006 elections, barred presidential hopeful General Fidy Andrianafidisoa attempted to stage a military coup to derail Ravalomanana's electoral campaign. The coup failed to materialize, and he was later arrested. Ravalomanana managed to secure a second five-year term in December 2006. He then launched the Madagascar Action Plan in 2007, which envisions reducing poverty levels 50 percent by 2012, developing global partnerships for economic growth, and ensuring environmental sustainability.

When Didier Ratsiraka came to power in 1975, he attempted to create a personality cult through the publication of the Charter of the Socialist Revolution for Madagascar, popularly called the Boky Mena, or Red Book, in much the same way as Colonel Muammar Qaddafi had done in Libya with his Green Book.

GOVERNMENT

FROM ITS EARLIEST HISTORY up to 1975, Madagascar has seen the rule of independent kingdoms, such as the Merina and Menabe; defeat and control by a European colonial power (France); supposed independence as a republic (while still under French domination); autocratic wielding of power by President Philibert Tsiranana; and the introduction of a Marxist one-party state by President Didier Ratsiraka. The political theory of Marxism holds that, ideally, a country progresses from allegiance to a local ruler (feudalism) to privately owned production (capitalism) to public ownership of a country's assets (socialism) to the eventual goal of a classless society (Communism).

In Madagascar Communism brought economic ruin. Although President Ratsiraka instituted some private sector reforms in the late 1980s in a bid to curb government debt, growing dissatisfaction persisted among the public with the country's political and economic conditions. This eventually led, in 1992, to a new constitution, the creation of a multiparty political system, and reduced executive powers for the president. Economic decline continued, however, and the unhappy public called for a military government in early 1996. Ratsiraka's successor, President Albert Zafy, was impeached, allowing Ratsiraka to pull off a comeback in the election of February 1997. He then won a referendum to expand presidential power. In the 2001 presidential election, Ratsiraka was overthrown by Marc Ravalomanana. Today, under President Ravalomanana, Madagascar is a democratic republic with a free market economy.

Above: **Malagasy soldiers presenting arms at a military camp in Antananarivo.**

Opposite: **Polling station workers ready for voters in the 2006 elections in Antananarivo.**

A small coastal community of *côtiers*. Those coastal people, or *côtiers*, were far less advantaged than the Merina prior to French rule in Madagascar.

THE CHANGING CONSTITUTION

Annexed by France as a colony in 1896, the Malagasy Republic, as it was then called, became self-governing in 1958. The island gained full independence in 1960 and changed its name to the Democratic Republic of Madagascar in 1975. Ruled by President Didier Ratsiraka as La Deuxième République, meaning the Second Republic, from 1975 to 1992, Madagascar tried to adopt Marxism, nationalizing foreign banks and firms.

Under the 1975 constitution, there was a People's National Assembly, with 137 members elected by the people. Nevertheless, a 22-member Supreme Revolutionary Council, two-thirds of whom were appointed by the president, made the most important decisions. For practical matters of administration, the president appointed a Council of Ministers that was headed by the prime minister. Those 17 years are now regarded as a dictatorship. A new constitution, ratified in August 1992, introduced a more democratic government and several political parties were formed. In 1998 the constitution was amended to strengthen the presidency. Changes included the expansion of presidential power to handpick one-third of the senators and the removal of the legislature's control over the prime minister and cabinet. More revisions were made to the constitution in April 2007, including the creation of 22 smaller regions to replace the six autonomous regions and the enlargement of presidential powers in cases of emergency.

According to Madagascar's current constitution, the president is the head of state and the prime minister is the head of government. The president holds executive power. The parliament is bicameral, consisting of the National Assembly and the Senate. The Senate has 90 members, two-thirds of whom are elected by local legislators, with the remainder appointed by the president. The power to create legislation rests with both the Senate and the National Assembly, which consists of 160 members serving under the prime minister.

Traditionally there were three levels of society in Madagascar that seemed almost feudal—nobles, freemen, and workers. These divisions vanished long ago, but those living on the high plateau (largely of Merina descent) have always considered themselves superior, while those in the coastal areas, the *côtiers*, often felt deprived of power and education. When Madagascar gained its independence, however, the departing French had ensured that the government was dominated by *côtiers*, and since then, a conscious effort has been made to keep the Merina elite from swooping back into power.

Madagascar is a member of the United Nations and the African Union. Foreign donors heavily influence its current political environment. In 2002 donor countries pledged $1 billion over a period of five years as a demonstration of their confidence in Madagascar's new government. It received further help in 2006 from the African Development Bank in the form of a $52 million loan, and Madagascar continues to maintain its political and economic stability. Madagascar adheres to policies of the World Bank and the IMF in creating development zones around urban centers, resulting in ongoing decentralization and liberalization.

NATIONAL DEFENSE

Since 1975, Madagascar's army, navy, air force, and police have been incorporated into one body, the People's Armed Forces—consisting of the army, 12,500-strong; navy, 500, including 100 marines; air force, 500; and the National Gendarmerie, a military body charged with police duties that is 8,100-strong. Madagascar has no need for a large military force, so its small army is used mainly for maintaining law and order in conjunction with

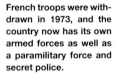

French troops were withdrawn in 1973, and the country now has its own armed forces as well as a paramilitary force and secret police.

the gendarmes. Officially, there is compulsory military service of 18 months for males, but not all conscripts are called up. Madagascar reportedly also has an East German–trained secret police. The air force operates 12 combat aircraft that include fighters and helicopters from North Korea as well as Cessnas (small, piston-powered aircraft) and transport planes.

Both police and army personnel wear camouflage khaki uniforms and can be difficult to distinguish from one another. The police usually wear a blue kepi, a cap with a flat circular top and a visor that used to be worn in the French military, while soldiers often have red or black berets.

JUSTICE AND ADMINISTRATION

The judicial system is still modeled after that of France. It includes the Supreme Court in Antananarivo, the High Constitutional Court, and the Court of Appeal. There are eleven courts of first instance for civil and commercial cases, and ordinary criminal courts in most towns for criminal cases. Most judges and magistrates have had French training, but the traditional law of the Merina and other ethnic groups is taken into account by state magistrates when judging marriage, family, land, and inheritance cases.

Police officers on duty. The Malagasy system of law and justice is based on French codes and practices.

Local government includes 22 *faritra* (FAR-trr), meaning districts, that are subdivided into 116 prefectures and again subdivided into 1,548 smaller counties and 16,969 localized community rule called *fokontany* (FOOK-on-TAN). An elected council governs each level. Unfortunately, political change combined with a faltering economy has not provided reliable justice. There are instances where government officials starved

President Marc Ravalomanana, who is serving his second term in 2008, has brought many popular changes to the people of Madagascar.

of funds may turn a blind eye to smuggling or major fraud, as was the case in October 2006 when 16 noncommissioned military officers and gendarmes were apprehended in Diégo-Suarez for their involvement in the trafficking of handguns, grenades, and AK-47s. There are also suspicions that criminal gangs may receive protection from law enforcers. To combat the problem of corruption, the government adopted new anticorruption laws in 2004. This included the establishment of BIANCO—the Independent Anti-Corruption Bureau—to improve the image of the local police and judiciary that are often perceived as too inefficient and corrupt to administer justice.

STATUS TODAY

Under Didier Ratsiraka, Madagascar astonishingly turned from authoritarian socialism to liberal democracy, but the island remained deeply in debt, and industrial and foreign investment declined drastically. Ratsiraka's successor, Albert Zafy, rejected the International Monetary Fund's (IMF) proposal of an austerity plan because he considered it too drastic on an island "where nearly half the children suffer retarded growth or acute malnutrition." This did not stop him from running up a bill of some $10 million in April 1995 for a fleet of coastal patrol boats from Israel and for the training of 500 personal security guards. Zafy's popularity declined, and as the country's economy deteriorated, the increasingly disgruntled public called for a military government in early 1996. In June 1996 the legislature impeached Zafy for corruption and exceeding his powers. In November 1996 Madagascar held a presidential election and Didier Ratsiraka, the previous

THE PRESIDENT

The president is elected by the vote of the people for a term of five years, while the prime minister is appointed by the president and handles the day-to-day running of the country together with the Council of Ministers. The president also has the power to dissolve the National Assembly, the lower chamber of the Madagascan parliament. In July 2007 the intention to dissolve the National Assembly before the end of May 2008 was announced, a move deemed necessary to adapt to the country's new constitutional changes. One such change includes the reduction of parliamentarians from 160 to 127. As the *ray aman-dreny* (ray AH-mahn-dray-n), a traditional title previously reserved for the king, the president shall ensure respect for the constitution and be responsible for national sovereignty and integrity. The person of the president is also the symbol of national unity.

president deposed by Professor Zafy, was returned to power with 51 percent of the final vote.

Government corruption was rife under Ratsiraka also, and the public challenged his credibility. Inevitably, he lost the December 2001 presidential election to Marc Ravalomanana. President Ratsiraka demanded a run-off. Ravalomanana rejected the suggestion and declared himself president-elect. The High Institutional Court, however, ordered a recount. Public support for Ravalomanana grew, and he called for a general strike on February 4, 2002. Ratsiraka responded by declaring a state of emergency and blockaded the capital from receiving food and fuel. Five governors of the then six administrative provinces declared themselves autonomous in the ensuing crisis.

The recount organized by the African Union declared that Ravalomanana was indeed the winner, and he was sworn in on May 6, 2002. The six-month standoff between Ravalomanana and Ratsiraka had terrible economic repercussions for the already-ailing island. The IMF estimated that the strikes had cost the country $14 million a day. It took Ravalomanana's government two years to return the economy to its preconflict level. He also recaptured the five secessionist provinces, abolished them, and divided the country into 22 regions. Today, expectations remain high for Ravalomanana and his political party, the Tiako I Madagasikara, which means "I love Madagascar," or TIM for short, to lead Madagascar to political and economic success. In 2008 he was elected to a second term as Madagascar's president.

Before he became president of Madagascar, Marc Ravalomanana was a self-made dairy tycoon who started out selling homemade yogurt off the back of a bicycle.

ECONOMY

ACCORDING TO THE HUMAN Development Index of 2006, an indicator or list measuring life expectancy, educational attainment, and standard of living, Madagascar was ranked 143rd out of 177 countries. Following a slow yet steady World Bank and IMF-led campaign of privatization and liberalization, Madagascar's economic progress in recent years has been strong, recording a growth rate of 4.7 percent in 2006. Its gross national product (GNP) is estimated at $17.27 billion, and inflation fell from about 40 percent a decade ago to 12 percent in 2006. The island's efforts at reviving the economy were recognized by donor countries that cancelled Madagascar's $161 million debt in 2001. Likewise, the World Bank and the International Monetary Fund wrote off about $2 billion of Madagascar's debt in 2004, when tropical cyclones left thousands of residents homeless. In April 2005 Madagascar became the first recipient of aid under the U.S. Millennium Challenge Account. That is a $110 million four-year package aimed at reducing poverty, strengthening the country's banking and financial sector, and promoting investment in agriculture. More than 70 percent of Madagascar's population lives below the poverty line. Although it will take some time for Madagascar to restore investor confidence, its economic outlook looks promising.

Above: **Brick making using locally available clay, leaving the bricks to dry in the sun, like adobe.**

Opposite: **Women working in rice plantations, historically a life-sustaining crop involving tremendous hand labor.**

ECONOMIC IMPROVEMENT

Before 1972, following the French colonial style, the government established producers' cooperatives that collected and processed most of the rice harvested in the country. The farmers were paid extremely low prices that

The busy capital city of Antananarivo is where most business transactions take place.

they resented bitterly. The disquiet over this important crop led to domestic turbulence and a shift in economic policy.

The post-1975 military regime attempted to introduce a "socialist paradise," and formerly French-dominated firms were nationalized. The government also created state monopolies for import-export trading, and the textile, cotton, and power industries became regulated. In spite of these resolute measures, the economy declined, and the poorest people were hit the hardest. The rural population struggled to survive day by day, bartering with cattle and bags of coarse rice. By 1982 Madagascar was technically bankrupt.

In June 1990 France wrote off Madagascar's debt of 4 billion French francs in response to moves by President Didier Ratsiraka to accept a free-market economy, which included disbanding agricultural marketing boards and diversifying traditional primary exports. The economy did not revive straightaway, but from 1997 to 2001 solid economic growth was seen, with foreign investments, further privatizations, and the development of an export processing zone (EPZ) where tariffs and quotas were eliminated, contributing to the slow-growing success.

This success was unhappily derailed by the six-month political crisis over the disputed outcome of the presidential elections in December 2001. Economic activity came to a halt when Ratsiraka's forces blockaded the capital, damaging the growing industrial sector. Foreign investment fell away sharply, and a recovery plan had to be instituted in mid-2002 to salvage donor countries' confidence. Presented at a World Bank "Friends of Madagascar" conference, the plan included interventions in health, education, and rural development. The modernization of the land transportation network and the rehabilitation and maintenance of roads also moved to center stage. It took President Ravalomanana two years to reverse the economic slippage caused by the conflict.

Over 200 investors, particularly garment manufacturers, have profited from the island's tax breaks. As a result, the export of apparel to European and U.S. markets has boomed. To ensure continued foreign investments, President Ravalomanana launched the five-year Madagascar Action Plan in 2007 that includes steps for fighting corruption by implementing a Code of Conduct for all public employees and by increasing the funding of anticorruption institutions.

Other aims include encouraging the study of American and European business techniques as well as the promotion of full employment for the Malagasy. Projected aims include setting up centers for employment counseling and training in the 22 regions as well as developing a vocational training program.

Experienced workers sort through vanilla pods at a production site in Anjombalava. Vanilla is one of Madagascar's most successful exports.

TRADE AND INDUSTRY

Trade is precariously unbalanced, with imports (textiles, food, chemicals, machinery, and petroleum) being valued at almost double that of exports (coffee, vanilla, sugar, and cotton cloth). More than a third of all exports go to France and another third to the United States. Germany and Japan are two of Madagascar's other key trading partners. Local industry consists largely of factories processing agricultural products (such as flour, tapioca, rice, wood, paper pulp, cotton, fertilizer, oils, sugar, cigarettes and tobacco, and sisal rope and mats) or manufacturing textiles, mostly in or around Antananarivo. The production of cement and other consumer items like soap and beer dominate the industrial sector. Mining production includes graphite, chromite, and mica. Other resources include titanium ore, low-grade iron ore, low-grade coal, some nickel, and copper, though these have not been exploited.

There is a variety of semiprecious stones, but none of great value. On land and offshore, oil has been discovered. It is expected that Madagascar will start exporting crude oil in the next few years. Toamasina, which has a deepwater harbor, is Madagascar's main port. The oil refinery there has a production capacity of 200,000 tons (1.47 million barrels) a year, with 30,000 tons (about 220,000 barrels) for local consumption and 170,000 tons (1.25 million barrels) for export. Mahajanga is accessible only to small ships, but has considerable traffic with its neighboring African nation, the Comoros, an island group northwest of Madagascar. Antsiranana (Diégo-Suarez) has one of the world's finest natural harbors and was once used

VANILLA

Madagascar (together with Réunion and the Comoros islands) used to supply 80 percent of the world's vanilla. Now most of the crop goes to the United States, where it is used by the ice cream industry and in the making of cola drinks (in which vanilla is an essential ingredient). Today Madagascar provides half of the world's supply of vanilla, exporting about 1,000 tons a year. In recent years there has been a boom in vanilla prices. In 2003, 2.2 pounds (1 kg) of vanilla was sold for as much as 2 million Malagasy ariary, the currency of Madagascar, or $124. Unfortunately, this boom was followed by a spate of vanilla-related thefts, murders, and poaching.

Vanilla is grown mostly on the hot, wet east coast where vanilla orchids (originally from Mexico) are pollinated by hand. Nine months later the seedpods will be 6 to 8 inches (15 to 20 cm) long. They are picked, blanched in vats of boiling water, then dried in the sun for about five months.

as a French naval base, but it is located far from the other main economic centers.

The Malagasy banking system is made up of the Central Bank, which was formed in 1973, and six other commercial banks. All commercial and banking organizations were nationalized in 1975 but privatized again in 1988. The commercial banks include the Malagasy Bank of the Indian Ocean, set up in September 1990 as part of a general bank privatization program, and the Compagnie Malgache de Banque, created by Malagasy private operators.

There are eight central trade unions, which include the Union des Syndicats d' Intérêt Économique de Madagascar, the Union des Syndicats Autonomes de Madagascar, and the Sendika Kristianina Malagasy.

AGRICULTURE

Madagascar's economy is largely based on agriculture, which employs close to 80 percent of the workforce but accounts for less than 30 percent of its GDP.

A grower drying his produce in the sun. The island enjoys a year-round abundance of locally grown spices like cloves, vanilla, and pepper.

Because the countryside is mountainous, only 5 percent of the land is actually farmed. The main crops are rice, cassava, sugarcane, cloves, coffee, and vanilla. Overseas markets are unreliable, so there is frequent overproduction and stockpiling. Rice occupies about 60 percent of the land under cultivation.

Sugarcane is farmed in plantations in the northwest and along the east coast. Cassava, potatoes, and yams are grown in the highlands. Corn does well only on the central plateau. Bananas are grown commercially on the

Humped zebu cattle are raised for food, but they are also useful for plowing the land.

east coast. Many farmers also grow carrots, haricot beans (kidney beans), tomatoes, and other vegetables. There is a small but steady production of wine, the pride of local vineyards. Sisal plantations do well in the arid south, but the fiber factories discharge an acidic green juice extracted from the crushed sisal leaves. This juice is often dumped into rivers, causing oxygen depletion of the water.

CATTLE AND FISHING

Zebu cattle, which presumably were introduced from Africa, are of great importance in Madagascar. The humped animals are symbolic of wealth and are used in religious sacrifice as well as for transportation and plowing. Since it is considered more desirable to have a large number of thin cows than a small number of fat ones, the quality of local cattle remains poor, making it difficult to breed them for meat consumption or export. Other domestic animals are sheep, goats, pigs, chickens, geese, and turkeys. The Malagasy consider their wild animals, such as the lemurs, of little

importance, although they are beginning to realize that tourists who show an interest in the creatures are a source of revenue.

There was a cotton boom between 1982 and 1986, but farmers who benefited from the high export prices viewed it as a short-lived windfall, because cotton is largely grown for the local textile industry and is not a leading export cash crop like coffee, vanilla, and cloves. So they frittered away their new prosperity on endless rounds of festivities.

Although fishing has been relatively slow to develop as an industry, fish products in recent years have become significant sources of export revenue. Madagascar allows four joint-venture companies and vessels from the European Union to conduct commercial fishing in exchange for compensation. French investment has also helped establish a tuna cannery. Inland, irrigated rice fields are stocked with breeding fish, although the catch is used mainly for local consumption. Tourist hotels offer good quality seafood that includes tuna, plaice (flounder), lobster, crab, calamari (squid), and prawns.

A woman carrying her child while planting rice in the ashes of a felled slash-and-burn area of Ranomafana's forest.

FORESTRY

Forests cover 22 percent of the land surface and contain many valuable hardwoods, such as ebony, rosewood, and sandalwood, while gums, resins, and plants used in tanning and dyeing and for medicinal purposes are found in many wooded places. Farming people need open land to cultivate rice and to pasture their goats and cattle, however, so they cut down the trees unsparingly.

The timber is used to supply 82 percent of household fuel, either in the form of logs or as charcoal, and as a result, the amount of forested land shrinks alarmingly every year. Most of the wood and charcoal used for fuel is illegally obtained, taken from supposedly protected areas. This ceaseless deforestation allows the valuable topsoil to be washed away.

Although there are many narrow valleys with fast-flowing waterfalls, only a small number have been harnessed for hydroelectric power. Yet somehow the seven existing power stations are able to meet 63.9 percent of the country's electrical needs. Thermal plants are another source of power. Bottled propane gas is often used for cooking.

"Madagascar, the world's best-kept secret."

—Tourist slogan devised by Herizo Razafimahaleo, former Minister of Tourism and Industry.

46

TOURISM

Madagascar has much to offer tourists, and if the facilities and marketing were improved, the economy might enjoy immense benefits. But the islands of Mauritius and the Seychelles lure visitors away with their better hotels and transportation services. The real attractions of Madagascar are its unique flora and fauna and the friendliness of its people. Until roads, transportation services, and accommodations are improved, however, the majority of tourists will be hardy travelers prepared to rough it out.

Specially created reserves such as Périnet (east of Antananarivo) and Berenty or Kaleta Park (in the south) are proving to be beneficial to tourists and local residents alike. In the parks, wildlife can be viewed easily along walking trails where lemurs will tumble out of the trees at the wave of a banana. They stand momentarily upright and then dance sideways, tail looped high, looking perpetually surprised. The parks also provide employment for wardens, guides, and maintenance staff.

Trees and rare wildlife are being preserved—provided thieves do not gain access first. There are also ecological tourism centers that offer audiovisual explanations of the areas, like the one at Andohahela near Tôlañaro. The islands of Nosy Be and Nosy Boraha are sprucing up, too, and are becoming increasingly popular with overseas visitors for the scuba diving and snorkeling that showcase some of the most beautiful coral reefs in the region. Nosy Boraha also provides whale-watching tours, as migrating humpback whales gather off the island to breed from July to September.

A tourist scaling the rock face of a cliff in Andringitra National Park.

47

Air Madagascar provides both domestic and international service, with supplemental flights by several foreign airlines.

COMMUNICATION

No one will deny that the island's road transportation system is in a poor state. Only some 11 percent of the roads are paved, and most of those are full of potholes. The other roads are dirt trails that are often impassable in the wet season. In theory, the Malagasy drive on the right-hand side of the road, but in fact they drive wherever there are any visible fragments of hard surface. They drive their vehicles (most of them French) very carefully, partly out of courtesy to other motorists but mainly because replacement parts are almost impossible to find. Most people travel by oxcart or *taxi-brousse* (TAK-see-BROOSS), a minibus or pickup truck.

Flying is the favored way to travel for those who can afford it, and the Malagasy wear their best clothes for their trips: ladies in fine dresses and men in smart shirts. The national airline was originally called Mad Air, until somebody thought it disrespectful. They renamed it Air Madagascar, so now it is known as Air Mad. Air France, Air Mauritius, and France's Corsair fly in from abroad. There is an international airport at Antananarivo and 29 other airfields with paved runways in most major towns around the island.

Much of the transportation system centers on Antananarivo, and the facilities serve the slightly richer areas of the high plateau and the ports on the east coast. There are only two railway lines that connect the plateau with the east coast: one links Fianarantsoa to the port of Manakara, and the other runs from Antananarivo to Toamasina. Each seldom runs more than one train a day. The line from Antananarivo to Toamasina is 235 miles (378 km) long. Built between 1901 and 1913, it is both a scenic wonder and a considerable engineering feat. To improve Madagascar's rail system, the government granted Mandarail a 25-year concession to operate the national railroad. Operations began in 2003. The Pangalanes Canal offers a waterway of lagoons linked by canals along the east coast, but it is poorly maintained and only isolated stretches are usable.

The postal system does its best but is hardly reliable. There are only about 66,900 telephones and 325,000 television sets for the estimated population of 19.4 million. There are also 504,700 cell phone users. Madagascar has two Internet service providers for its 90,000 users.

THE FUTURE

Madagascar's economic survival seems to be based on maintaining a balance between preserving its forests and rare flora and fauna (thus attracting tourism and support from environmental organizations) and finding some way of stimulating its trade and capitalizing on its mineral resources. Although poverty touches every corner of the island, with 70 percent of its people living on $1 a day, Ravalomanana's spirited leadership hints at a more optimistic economic forecast. Strategic alliances with private investors and financial institutions have been made, and in a bid to reduce poverty levels by half in the next five years, other economic measures have been undertaken. President Ravalomanana had a successful first term implementing free-market reforms and canceling foreign debts. His second term appears set to renew his initial success in improving the country's economic growth and the people's quality of life.

A Western missionary surveys the lives of the common people in Madagascar, in hopes that this study will help create a better future for future Madagasy.

49

ENVIRONMENT

MADAGASCAR IS RENOWNED FOR ITS beauty and tremendous biodiversity. Over 200,000 known species of flora and fauna have made the island their home, living in habitats ranging from the rugged mountains in the north to the spiny desert in the south and to the lush rain forests, rolling hills, and mangrove swamps in between. Some 150,000 of these species are not found anywhere else on the planet. Regrettably, the arrival of humans and their subsequent colonization have led to the long and unrelenting process of degradation and extinction of the island's wondrous plant and animal life.

Conservation of Madagascar's natural ecosystem is vitally important, and the 2007 Madagascar Action Plan has boldly outlined numerous strategies for the sustainable development and protection of its natural resources. The government has a long hard campaign ahead, not only with regard to improving the living standards of its citizens but also to wildlife preservation and environmental sustainability.

EXHAUSTED SOIL

In Madagascar 80 percent of the people are dependent on the island's natural resources for sustenance. The island's economy is largely based on agriculture. Unfortunately, the people think that it is an economic necessity for them to clear away forest cover to grow rice and cassava, to keep up charcoal production, and to burn bushes to maintain pastureland for grazing their goats and prized zebu cattle. Every year as much as a third of Madagascar's remaining 32 million acres (13 million ha) of forest are burned to sustain these practices.

Above: **These canyons are created by devastating soil erosion, due to slash-and-burn forest clearance.**

Opposite: **The physical landscape of Madagascar glows with its rich rice fields and granite domes.**

Slash-and-burn farming in Madagascar is normally practiced when converting tropical rain forests to rice fields. Usually an acre or two (0.4 or 0.8 ha) of forest is cut, burned, and later planted with rice. Such techniques can yield rice production for about two years before the field must be left to lie fallow (dormant) for the next four to six years. Rice is then cultivated again for two or three more cycles. By the third cycle, the soil is usually too stripped of essential nutrients to support further rice farming. Scrub vegetation and wild grasses then overrun the tired soil. Soil erosion becomes a problem, especially during heavy rains, because, unlike trees, these alien vegetations cannot anchor the soil well.

Madagascar loses so much soil to erosion—about 180 tons per acre per year—that its rivers run bloodred, causing huge stains in the surrounding Indian Ocean. About 80 percent of the country's original vegetation has already been destroyed, and today much of the country is sterile grassland, with arable land making up only 5 percent of the total land area.

Soil erosion brings with it a host of other problems, most of which threaten the way of life of the people. Surrounding water becomes undrinkable as it is polluted with silt, fisheries suffer as fish roes are smothered with soil sediments, and floods become increasingly devastating as siltation raises the riverbeds. Transportation networks disintegrate because roads that cut across forests become dangerously impassable. The Malagasy people are not alone in suffering the effects of these agricultural practices—the island's plant and animal species are also affected.

ENDANGERED FLORA AND FAUNA

Madagascar has one of the richest and most unique assortment of flora and fauna in the world, and 85 percent of its flora and a majority of its fauna—39 percent of birds, 91 percent of reptiles, 99 percent

of amphibians, and 100 percent of lemurs are endemic, native, to the country. It can therefore be considered an ecological catastrophe that so much of Madagascar's flora and fauna are being driven to the brink of extinction as a result of deforestation, forest fires, and overgrazing that can lead to desertification.

In 2007 the World Conservation Union listed 37 of Madagascar's major fauna as critically endangered, 88 as endangered, and 137 as vulnerable. This list includes 47 of the island's threatened mammalian species. The mammals include the golden-crowned sifaka lemur, the hairy-eared dwarf lemur, and the humpback whale. Some 35 bird species and 280 plant species are also endangered.

The lucrative worldwide market for endangered animal products, such as snake leather and tortoise shells, has led to the further decimation of animal habitats. The rare plowshare tortoise in northeast Madagascar can bring an estimated $30,000 on the black market. Looting and smuggling of such species for a short-term cash gain poses a long-term danger of serious ecological imbalance.

The plowshare tortoises found in Madagascar are examples of one of the most endangered species in the world.

Russell Mittermeier, the president of Conservation International, visits the Nosy Mangabe Reserve.

CONSERVATION

The government is committed to protecting Madagascar's rich ecological heritage. In 2003 it pumped about $18 million into the protection and conservation of Madagascar's environment, and there are plans to increase this amount to $50 million by 2012. Foreign donors and other international organizations are also lending Madagascar a hand in the protection of its environment. The World Bank has helped to sponsor Madagascar's 60 protected areas, including nature reserves and national parks. The World Wildlife Fund (WWF) is partnering with Madagascar to carry out several ecological projects, as are the Durell Wildlife Conservation Trust from the United Kingdom, the Missouri Botanical Gardens, the Duke University Primate Center, the United Nations Development Programme (UNDP), and the Malagasy nongovernmental organization FANAMBY, to name just a few.

At the fifth World Parks Congress in 2003, President Marc Ravalomanana promised to more than triple the size of Madagascar's protected areas from 4.2 million acres (1.7 million ha) to 14.8 million acres (6 million ha) by 2008. The island's marine-area coverage will also be expanded from half a million acres (200,000 ha) to 2.5 million acres (1 million ha). Formerly maintained by the National Association for the Management of Protected Areas (ANGAP), these significant tracts have been under the responsibility of the System of Protected Areas of Madagascar (SAPM) since 2006. Such specified zones safeguard identified threatened species and ecosystems. Access to these areas is open only for authorized scientific research. Even national parks open to the public are supervised to prevent abuse. A visitor must obtain a permit to visit the parks, must be accompanied by a guide, and is allowed to walk only along prescribed trails.

The Malagasy themselves understand that the island's natural environment is fragile and needs to be protected. But the practical need to feed their growing families is even greater than the need for environmental conservation. For conservation to be successful, the government must

"Our government intends to make protection of the precious environment of Madagascar one of our highest priorities."

—President Marc Ravalomanana to the UN General Assembly, September 2002

MADAGASCAR'S MEGAFAUNA

Before man set foot on Madagascar over 2,000 years ago, there lived on the island huge tortoises, giant predatory raptors (whose eggs were said to be big enough to make an omelet to feed 150 people), pygmy hippopotamuses, and enormous lemurs, the largest of which had the body mass of a male gorilla. These endemic animals were the biggest animals on the island—the megafauna. Explorations at cave, marsh, and stream sites have shown that competition with man for food, habitat, and space led to the gradual annihilation of the megafauna. Also found were subfossils of at least 17 extinct species of lemurs. Sharp cuts and chop marks characteristic of skinning and filleting were found on lemur bones, evidence that humans ate them into extinction.

Although these titans no longer walk among man, their remains nonetheless provide compelling examples of the staggering and distinctive biodiversity that make up Madagascar.

Losing an acre of forest in Madagascar has more serious repercussion on the world's biodiversity than losing an acre of forest elsewhere in the world.

reconcile the immediate needs of the people with the long-term benefits that conservation can yield. Good socioeconomic practices need to be implemented to generate a sustainable environment.

With this in mind, the government has drafted strategies to establish more land reserves for reforestation. Currently, reforested areas cover 890,000 acres (360,000 ha) of land. It is hoped that by 2012 the areas will be increased to 1.3 million acres (530,000 ha).

To decrease the dependence on charcoal, the government is also encouraging the use of biofuels such as palm oil, jatropha plants, soy, and sugarcane as alternative energy resources.

Rice cultivation is a deeply ingrained cultural practice, and new techniques of cultivation may take a while to catch on. One method of restoring degraded land is through using the permaculture system of

This rain forest in Madagascar has been destroyed for road building and timber.

developing efficient ecosystems by planting *savoka* (sah-VOOK) gardens consisting of a mixture of carefully selected native forest plants and fruits or vegetable plants cultivated on fallow plots of land. These plants not only enrich the soil they also yield a steady stream of food crops. Ginger, for example, adds phosphorus to the soil, while leguminous plants (peas and beans) reintroduce lost nitrogen. Other plants such as vanilla, banana, coffee, and rubber also help to restore lost nutrients. Such sustainable use of soil can help in maintaining biological diversity and the preservation of Madagascar's forests for decades.

Ecotourism and teaching about the environment in schools are other moves to encourage and raise national awareness of environmental conservation practices.

A Malagasy man holds the egg of the extinct aepyornis, a flightless bird that once lived in Madagascar. **Conservation of the natural environment is important to every Malagasy.**

ECOLOGICAL TREATIES

The preservation of the environment is an ongoing battle in Madagascar. As early as 200 years ago, the Merina king Andrianampoinimerina recognized the need to protect the island's great trees. He punished those who deforested large swaths of land, but the practice continued. The island's efforts to protect its ecology legally began with the French in 1927. The colonial government established 10 reserves to halt the ever-diminishing forest cover. This proved unsuccessful as well. Effective conservation gained momentum only in the late 1980s when Madagascar worked with the WWF to evaluate all the protected areas in the country and to provide people living near the reserves with economically viable alternatives to many destructive customs.

While small-scale fishing is largely unregulated, Madagascar authorities have established tight control over the fishing activities in deeper waters in a move to protect the diverse range of marine life.

Today Madagascar is member to a long list of agreements and treaties relevant to conservation. International treaties include the Convention on International Trade in Endangered Species (CITIES), Convention on Biological Diversity (CBD), the Ramsar Convention on the Protection of Wetlands, the Indian Ocean–South East Asian Marine Turtle Memorandum of Understanding (IOSEA), and the agreement for the establishment of the Indian Ocean Tuna Commission. It is also party to the Convention on Fishing and Conservation of Living Resources of the High Seas. Moreover, in January 2007 the island began its partnership with the Convention on the Conservation of Migratory Species of Wild Animals (CMS).

Madagascar adheres to the measures set out by the African Convention with regard to conservation of nature and natural resources. It also signed a convention concerning its protected areas and wild flora and fauna,

PROTECTED AREAS IN MADAGASCAR

Areas of biological, archaeological, or cultural significance are placed under protection in Madagascar. There are six categories of protected areas, one of which is the state-declared Strict Nature Reserve where entering or camping is forbidden. As more nature reserves become national parks, however, the distinction between the six categories is becoming increasingly blurred. The other five categories are the national parks, special reserves, conservation sites, classified forests, and reforestation zones.

Protected areas that are categorized as Strict Nature Reserves include Bemaraha (north), Betampona, Lokobe, Tsaratanana, and Zahamena.

Madagascar's National Parks include Andohahela, Andringitra, Ankarafantsika, Baie de Baly, Bemaraha (south), Isalo, Kirindy Mitea, Mananara-Nord, Mantadia, Marojejy, Masaola, Midongy du Sud, Montagne d'Ambre, Ranomafana, Tsimanampetsotsa, Tsingy de Namoroka, Zahamena, and Zombitse Vohibasia.

Some of the more popular special reserves are Ankarana, Andranomena, Cap Sainte Marie, Beza-Mahafaly, and Nosy Mangabe.

The category conservation sites was added in 2003. One such site is Makira, located in northeast Madagascar. The forests of Makira stand between the two protected areas of Masoala National Park and Anjanaharibe-Sud Special Reserve.

Classified forests include Andavakoera, Anjanaharibe, Bezavona, and Tsitongambarika.

Although the creation of reforestation zones was not directly related to the conservation of biological diversity, it was a necessary move to curtail soil erosion and the protection of Madagascar's water basins. There are currently 77 reforestation zones.

and another one for the protection, management, and development of the marine and coastal environment of the Eastern African region.

Other ecological treaties include the Agreement at Paris in 2006 to set up an international office to deal with contagious diseases of animals and the Kyoto Protocol on limiting global greenhouse gas emissions. Madagascar is also a member of the UN convention on combating desertification as well as climate change.

MALAGASY

IT WOULD BE HARD to find anywhere else in the world a population that is universally so genuinely friendly, gracious, and hospitable.

Many Malagasy are countryside and village people. For many centuries before the arrival of the Europeans, they lived in geographical isolation, trying to strengthen the mutual bonds of kinship by marrying within the family clan. That was their protection against the outside world, although they also incorporated refugees from other groups into their community.

Malagasy are characteristically hardworking, genial, and optimistic. The markets are busy, with well-worn money changing hands after spirited bargaining. Those with cars drive with consideration for others, and radios are not played at a high volume in public places. Life seems relaxed, and the general attitude is that "it is good to live here." Even

Left: **A young Malagasy boy paddling a traditional pirogue along the Pangalanes Canal.**

Opposite: **A smiling Malagasy girl displaying her painted face. The clay paint is used for both decorative purposes and protection from the hot sun.**

A man descended from the Vazimba clan standing among the limestone pinnacles known as *tsingy*.

the public demonstrations in 2002 to install Ravalomanana as the new president, which lasted six months and were attended by some 500,000 people, were peaceful and almost carnival-like.

ORIGINS

No one is certain how the original settlers arrived in Madagascar. There has also been no evidence of a Stone Age, although there are legends of a pygmy race occupying the center of the island. Tradition says that

"Scratch a Malagasy and the blood of many nations trickles out."

—Local saying

STATISTICS

Percentage of the population under 15: 43.9 percent
Life expectancy: 60.23 years for men and 64.1 years for women
Birthrate: 38.6 per 1,000
Deaths: 8.51 per 1,000 each year
Population density: 83 persons per square mile (32 per square km)
Urban population: 27 percent

the first inhabitants were Malayo-Polynesians who crossed the Indian Ocean from Indonesia and Southeast Asia more than 2,000 years ago. Perhaps they were the Vazimba, a pastoral clan who tended herds of cattle on the central plateau long before the Merina arrived.

Antananarivo was originally a Vazimba town called Analamangao, but nothing much is known about the place or the vanished people who lived there. Today, small groups descended from the Vazimba do live in the rocky *tsingy*—an irregular limestone or dolomite landscape with sinkholes, underground streams, and caverns.

After the arrival of the original Vazimba, more settlers landed. In later years, those early inhabitants mixed with African slaves; Arab, Indian, and Portuguese traders; and also French colonials to form the ethnic groups of the island today.

The modern inhabitants of Madagascar are called Malagasy in English or Malgache in French. Although the country is geographically close to Africa and included in most lists of African countries, Malagasy do not consider themselves Africans. Those living in the central highlands are mostly short and slim. They have straight black hair, light brown skin, dark eyes, and high cheekbones (indicative of their Malay or Indonesian origins). Along the coast, people are often strikingly tall and much darker, with curly hair, indicating their descent from later African immigrants.

A young woman of African origin living in Toamasina, along the eastern coast of Madagascar.

ETHNIC GROUPS

Scholars have classified the people of Madagascar into about 20 ethnic groups. These are not tribes but groups of mixed descent whose members tend to marry among their own ethnicities. The rather vague boundaries of

A Malagasy man from the western coastline town of Morondava, where most residents are descended from early immigrants of Malaya and Indonesia.

their homelands are based on the traditional boundaries of ancient kingdoms.

The largest such group is the Merina. They once ruled the island and even now represent 27 percent of the population. Merina means "elevated people," and although most live on the high plateau around Antananarivo, they have also settled in other parts of the island. There used to be three social groups: nobles, freemen, and workers, but such categories are no longer used in democratic Madagascar. The *famadihana* (fa-ma-DEE-an) ceremony of reburial—a ceremony in which tombs are reopened and the deceased's shroud replaced with a new one—originated with the Merina.

Another large group, making up approximately 9 percent of the population, is the Betsimisaraka, which literally means "inseparable multitude." The people were initially from several smaller indigenous groups that blended together. They settled along the east coast where they were subjected to the influence of Europeans, particularly 18th-century pirates who arrived by sailing ships. Highly superstitious, they still believe in ghosts, mermaids, and little wild men from the forest that they refer to as *kalamoro* (KAR-la-MOOR).

The Betsileo, meaning "the invincibles," is the next largest group at 12.7 percent, and they live on the central plateau south of Fianarantsoa and the region around Antananarivo. They are mainly rice growers and wood-carvers. Merina and Betsileo are mainly descendants of early Malayan and Indonesian immigrants.

Other important groups are the Tsimihety, meaning "those who do not cut their hair"; the Sakalava (people of the long valley); the Antandroy (people of the thornbush); the Tanala (people of the forest); the Antaimoro (people of the banks); and the Bara, whose name is of uncertain origin. Smaller groups include the Antanosy, the Antaifasy, the Sihanaka, the Antakarana, the Betanimena, the Bezanozano, and the Mahafaly.

GROWING POPULATION

Madagascar now has an ethnically diverse population of about 19.4 million. There are four non-Malagasy minority groups: French, Chinese, Comorian, and an economically significant Indo-Pakistani community numbering approximately 60,000. There are about 47,000 Chinese and 113,000 French citizens who live and work in Madagascar. The 24,000-strong Comorian group is reportedly unpopular because of their wealth and lifestyle that set them apart socially. There used to be a larger community of Comorians, but after violent clashes and race riots, many of them retreated to the Comoro Islands in December 1977. There are also small numbers of refugees in Madagascar.

The population is growing rapidly, with a high concentration on the central plateau around Antananarivo and a lower density on the southeast coast. The western area is sparsely populated. Some 44 percent of the national population is under the age of 15, and close to three-quarters live in the countryside.

Government policy no longer opposes any form of birth control, and contraceptives and birth control advice are available to the general public. Nonetheless, the population is increasing at an average rate of 3.01 percent per year, one of the highest rates in the world. This means

Although Madagascar is often considered to be part of the Africa continent, Malagasy are not Africans. They have a mixed ancestry of Indonesian, African, and other ethnic origins.

that the island's population is set to double every 30 years, which would indicate that the Malagasy are fast exceeding their country's capacity to feed and employ themselves. The present population of around 19.4 million is estimated to rise to 23.8 million by the year 2015 and as much as 43.5 million by 2050.

The Malagasy believe that children are gifts from God and must be welcomed. They believe that the more children one has, the greater is one blessed. It is quite normal for a family to have as many as 8 or 10 children, and 14 is considered a lucky number!

DRESS

The all-purpose garment is the *lamba* (LAM-ba), a length of silk or cotton worn around the shoulders togalike and often draped over the head like a shawl. The way the *lamba* is draped around a woman indicates whether she is single, married, or widowed. If one end hangs down the right side of the body, it indicates mourning. Along the west coast and in the far south women often also wear sarongs or loose skirts.

For the Merina, the *lamba* is usually made of white cotton, and it is draped across the left shoulder like a Roman toga. Women of other groups, such as the Sakalava and Antakarana, wear colorful cotton *lambas* that they use for carrying babies while shopping or working in the fields.

Men also wear *lambas*, either around the waist or tied in a knot on the shoulder. On special occasions they may wear the long *lamba mena* (LAM-ba MAIN), meaning red cloth (although it is seldom red) indicating authority. *Lamba mena* also refers to the shroud used to wrap a dead body. Muslims wear the clothes indicated by Islamic tradition: men wear somber colors and usually a brimless cap, while married women are fully robed.

Nowadays, another garment is worn under the *lamba*. Women may wear a long dress, and men may wear jeans or shorts that are nearly always paired with a hat, for hats are seen as a sign of respectability. Western-style clothes are common, too. Shorts, short-sleeved shirts, and dresses are typical everyday wear. The Betsileo wear four-cornered hats, the Merina favor rice-straw hats, and the Bara wear cone-shaped hats. Woven raffia hats are for sale in every market, and even the jaunty American baseball cap has made its way to Madagascar.

Although boys may wear nothing more than a pair of shorts, girls and women dress modestly, always covering their chests. All enjoy having their hair dressed. Some grease their hair with animal fat to make it shine. Others tie their hair back with a colored ribbon. Most hairstyles reflect happiness. When a person is in mourning, though, the hair is left to hang down uncombed and untidy.

A boy wearing the *lamba*, the traditional Malagasy wrap clothing.

LIFESTYLE

IN MADAGASCAR, AS ELSEWHERE in the world, there is a vast difference between the lifestyles of those with money and those without. The rich live in the same way the French did when the island was still a French colony; others eat only what they can grow or obtain by barter. An estimated 73 percent of Malagasy live in the countryside, growing rice, tending cattle, or doing other farming-related activities. Urban residents make up slightly more than a quarter of the population.

TOWN LIFE

The hilltops around Antananarivo are ringed by huge circles. These are the deep defensive ditches that once guarded fortified villages, some of which had gates made of solid wheels of stone. Present-day villagers do not need to defend themselves, and many have moved down the hillsides to be nearer to potable water. But some inhabitants are still wary of the outside world.

The biggest city in Madagascar is the nation's capital, Antananarivo. Not only is it the center of government, education, and the economy, it is also the capital of the region of Analamanga. The city fans outward; houses are built on hills and ridges, and fields cover the floor of every valley. The inhabitants consider themselves city dwellers, even though some may plant rice and make sun-dried mud bricks. Taxis and telephones, newspapers and schools, freshly baked bread (long, thin baguettes in the French style), and machinery are all easily accessible and available. Shops offer art, jewelry, cameras, and computers as in any other city in the world.

Above: **Wealthier families live in the Upper Town in Antananarivo, where the houses have steep, angled roofs.**

Opposite: **People crowded together in a train in the city of Antananarivo. Madagascar's only train service is an economic lifeline for the multitude of people living far from the eastern seacoast.**

69

The popular Zoma market in the bustling city of Antananarivo had hundreds of stalls set up under huge, white umbrellas. The Zoma was a social hub of the region, and many locals also went there to trade.

Richer families live in the Upper Town where the more expensive shops are located. Narrow streets alive with traffic twist their way between blocks of shops and houses two or three stories high. On the lower slopes is a sea of red walls, terra-cotta roof tiles, and rusty iron rooftops. An occasional white minaret and several church spires spring up in between.

Near the bright flowers and green lawns of the Place de l'Indépendence stand most of the governmental buildings, including the impressive President's Palace. The military guards, wearing scarlet berets, have sentry boxes painted with stripes of white, green, and red. ShopRite, the best supermarket in town, with a wide array of food, clothing, and imported goods, is also there.

The highest hill is crowned with the old Queen's Palace, called the Rova, which was gutted by a fire in 1995. There is also a miniature Greek temple that seems curiously out of place. The twisting road that plunges down the hillside passes tiny shops.

Brightly colored plastic, which does not rot, is replacing the soft, natural colors of wood in the towns. The capital city may be crowded, dusty, shabby, and busy, yet those who live in it are the lucky ones. They have easier access to health resources—although those are limited—and most of their children attend school.

COUNTRY LIVING

Much of Madagascar's countryside may seem remote and isolated. Whether people live beside lagoons, in the mountains, forests, or fields,

the lack of roads and telephones make communication very difficult. But underneath the simplicity of living in the rural regions is the resilient drive of their inhabitants. The Malagasy are committed to earning enough to survive. They may lead cattle to nearly dried-up water holes, pick and sort vanilla pods, paddle dugout canoes in search of fish, or offer handfuls of nuts to potential buyers. Farmers, involved with the yearlong cycle of rice growing, guide cattle around the fields to plow the mud. They then plant the rice seedlings, bending over flooded fields, tend to and weed the crop, and scythe the harvest. After that comes the work of pounding the rice in a wooden mortar. Most families grow only enough for their own needs but often have to sell part of that to obtain cash.

At the southern tip of the island, village people typically live in huts made of wood and leaves. The men work on a nearby sisal plantation or fish the lake in pirogues made of baobab wood. Their nets, which are hung out on trees to dry, use stones for weights and carved baobab wood, which is very light, for floats.

A family selling yogurt, eggs, and goat meat by the roadside.

71

While the women sift through the tangled, spiny scrub for edible roots, the children play on the water's edge, careful not to touch the poisonous pink jellyfish. Older youngsters keep an eye on their family's few chickens, goats, and pigs.

What good timber remains in Madagascar is under constant attack. In the absence of mechanized tools, woodcutters often use old methods. A two-man team will cut a trunk into planks, one man guiding the long saw from a high platform, the other below, pulling—and finding himself covered in sawdust. It is a hard way to earn a living.

Charcoal-burners use eucalyptus wood (the eucalyptus tree was introduced to replace the fast-disappearing forests), piling logs into stacks and leaving them to smolder under a cover of turf sods for a week. The resulting sacks of charcoal may be the only source of income for a whole village.

In some communities the village is the woman's place and the forest is the man's; so it is a man's job to collect wood and a woman's task to use it for cooking.

Soap balls made with fat rendered from the hump of zebu cattle.

FAMILY LIFE

The extended family has traditionally been the strength of Malagasy society. A family council that included the grandparents used to make decisions pertaining to children's upbringing, basing decisions on ideals such as family solidarity, respect for elders, and mutual help. Much of this has changed, however, and many Malagasy say that family life in the past was better than what it is now, the young were more respectful, and there was greater harmony. Today, the generation gap is being felt, and traditional family structure may not be able to withstand a more modern lifestyle.

As divorce is now fairly common, Madagascar has an increasing number of single-parent families. The old ideal of having "seven boys and seven girls" is proving impossible to accomplish. With a growing number of broken homes, children are sometimes sent out to work, and some become unfortunate victims of abuse. As of 2005, 13 percent of children younger than 14 years old were reportedly living separately from their biological parents. In Antananarivo, 10 percent of under-five deaths were the result of children abandoned as babies or left to fend for themselves.

Madagascar is also not spared the prevalent and worrying trend of modernized living as evident in many other parts of the world. Even when

A typical Malagasy mother and children, sitting together outside their house.

CATTLE

Several hundred years ago, African humpback zebu cattle were introduced to Madagascar. Today, a herd of these cattle represents a walking bank account advertising the owner's wealth and respectability. A person's importance in the local society is measured in cattle. When a man manages to earn more money, he buys more cattle. Putting money in a bank is not a popular idea. Yet the cattle's significance extends beyond wealth. The well-being of the herds of a village stands for the continuing health and prosperity of the whole group of people who own them. Fat humps show that the cattle are in peak condition—but quantity is still considered more important than quality! Since cattle are such an established sign of wealth, it is not surprising that cattle rustlers (people who steal cattle) are afoot, especially in the savannah plains of the west and the dry south.

More than 80 words in the Malagasy language describe the people's beloved cattle and every part of their horns, hump, and hide. Cows come in various colors, and each color means something different. White muzzles, for example, look like restricting nosebags, so the owner of cows with such muzzles is said to be unlikely to find prosperity. A dappled hide denotes uncertainty, whereas a hide all of one color—except black, as pure black means ruin, like black fields devastated by locusts—indicates solidarity. Black-and-white cattle seem safer.

Cattle are occasionally sacrificed to please the ancestors and are sold or sacrificed if someone is very ill, as an offering to make that person well again. After a funeral, horns will be put on the grave to show how many zebus were slaughtered for the feast and thereby how rich and important the deceased had been.

"The worst never happens in Madagascar."

—*Travel brochure*

the family is intact, parents have to work and are often not around to impart social values to their children. This increasing lack of communication is a prime cause of delinquency. Children left to their own devices may soon discover the world of drugs and petty crime. Many parents try to cope with this situation by adopting highly repressive and punitive attitudes, leading to conflict within the home.

DAILY SURVIVAL

Poverty is rife in the country and much remains to be done to address still persistent unemployment, housing scarcity, homelessness, rural education, and health-care problems. Governmental reforms have not yet relieved these conditions.

In parts of the parched countryside that receive no rain for seven or eight months in a row, survival is a life skill for both people and plants.

Spiky plants and succulents have found a way to live, and as well, humans have learned to survive. There seems hardly anywhere to live or anything to live on, and for many months of the year, it may be too hot to work. Still, people carry firewood, water, vegetables, logs, and bulging sacks of rice in the hope of making a sale whenever they can.

TRANSPORTATION PROBLEMS

"Madagascar is not an island but an archipelago" is a local saying that emphasizes the diversity of the people and the poor means of communication, as

Pousse-pousse, or rick-shaws, provide the main form of transportation in the towns. Equipped with air-filled tires, they are pulled silently through the streets.

if groups were isolated little islands in a chain. As part of their defense strategy, several precolonial kingdoms refused to build roads. Even today it seems as if the Malagasy do not want better roads because that might invite an invasion of people. Most trails are made of dirt or mud and are almost unusable after a rain. One favored Malagasy expression is *mandrevou* (MAND-dr-FOH), which means "bottomless mud." The few paved roads that exist are pocked with potholes, and road signs are unknown. This condition is improving, though, as many important roads are now in the process of being paved. Most travelers travel by air or "port hop" around the coast by boat.

Much of the street traffic consists of carts pulled by two zebu oxen roped to a wooden yoke, ramshackle bicycles, or sometimes a car or van. But there are two vehicles that are special to Madagascar. The first is the *pousse-pousse* (POOSS-POOSS) meaning "push-push," a cart for passengers or goods, pulled by one man. It is similar to the Chinese rickshaw. Antsirabe is Madagascar's *pousse-pousse* capital, where

75

A modern wedding procession in Madagascar.

Chinese laborers brought in to work on the railways probably introduced the idea.

The other special vehicle is called a *taxi-brousse* or "bush-taxi," usually a minibus or pickup truck. Almost any vehicle will serve the purpose, though most are minibuses. The *taxi-brousse* service is part of the Malagasy lifestyle. In theory, these vehicles ply the roads between towns according to a timetable, but in fact, one departs only when there are enough passengers to make the trip worthwhile. The more people who squeeze into the *taxi-brousse*, the better the pay for the driver.

MARRIAGE

Marriage is a celebration of the natural life process of choosing a partner and starting a family. Christians celebrate with Western-style ceremonies; those who adhere to older customs still negotiate a bride-price in cattle, money, and gifts. These are meant to help the prospective bride set up her new home, but brides' fathers play a strong role in negotiations and sometimes keep part of the money.

In exchange for these gifts, including the man's promise to build her a house, the woman is expected to provide the necessary household goods, including bedding and cooking pots. A trial marriage is encouraged. The minimum legal age for marriage is 18 for both men and women. If the potential bride and groom are between the ages of 14 and 17, the agreement of their parents and a judge's approval are required.

BIRTH

The birth of a baby is a time for rejoicing because God is seen to have been generous. A small celebratory ceremony is usually performed seven days after the birth of the baby. Many children are given a Christian name in church, as well as a traditional Malagasy name. The time of day at which a baby is born is considered important and is part of the child's fortune, or *vintana* (vin-TARN). A baby born at dawn is destined to be an industrious and good worker, one born at midday may rise in fortune like the sun, and one born in the afternoon sunlight should find golden riches. If the birth process is slow and at a time when the sun is setting, however, life's fortunes may be expected to fade away.

People make a living selling fruits, vegetables, and all sorts of recycled goods. These vendors are at the famous Zoma market, now demolished.

OFF TO MARKET

The market plays a central role in the lives of rural people, and every day is market day. It is common to walk 9 to 12 miles (15 to 20 km) to the nearest marketplace. People will haggle there for the necessities of life: rice, roots, vegetables, salt, kerosene, candles, plastic bowls, and water cans, some filled with *toaka gasy* (TOH-ka GASH), an illegal homemade rum. The unit of measure is the *kapoka* (ka-POOK), which is the amount of rice or other dry goods that will fill an empty condensed milk can. Hopeful shoppers sort through boxes of old pieces of machinery, bolts, wrenches, and rusted bicycle parts. Vendors wander with trays of fruit,

The government schools cater to all levels of education, especially within the cities.

flowers, footballs, or baskets of shells. In addition to shopping, the market serves as a social center where people catch up on gossip or continue the previous week's conversation. There are also gambling outlets for those who wish to try their luck.

The equivalent of fast-food stalls are vendors selling fried, spicy stuffed pastries known as *sambos* (SAM-bohs) or as samosas, banana fritters, or slices of coconut.

In the central square of the capital city there used to be a world-famous market called the Zoma, meaning Friday. It has been demolished to ease traffic congestion. There, under white umbrellas or draped awnings, all sorts of things were for sale: fruit, vegetables, eggs, dried fish, pungent spices, caged birds, used shoes, secondhand clothes, cassette tapes, sacks of charcoal, kitchen utensils, and cast-iron cooking pots. A supermarket now stands where Zoma once did. Several small markets, however, can still be found in the side streets, replete with aggressive salesmen and beggars.

EDUCATION

School is compulsory for all children from ages 6 to 14. Institutions of education beyond high school include the University of Antananarivo, the University of Fianarantsoa, technical schools, teacher-training colleges, and agricultural schools. Although there has been an increase in university enrollment, higher education is still inadequately developed. A major problem is that many subjects offered by universities are out of date and thus do not satisfactorily match the needs of potential employers. Private specialized institutions, on the other hand, have improved during the past decade, providing more current curricula for their students in business, languages, management, and computer science. Currently 3 percent of the population (260 students per 100,000 inhabitants) has enrolled for tertiary education.

Primary school enrollment has also gone up. At present the primary education completion rate stands at 57 percent. Private schools (such as those run by the Alliance Française) play a significant role in the educational system, catering to those unable to enter either government or mission schools.

As with so much else in Madagascar, there is a huge difference between educational opportunities in and around the capital and what unfolds in the rest of the country. In Antananarivo most young children attend school, but in more remote regions of the island, children contribute to the agricultural workforce rather than attend school. Schools are also severely short of teaching staff. On average, there are 52 students per teacher at the elementary level, making it difficult to teach effectively. Outlined under the Madagascar Action Plan 2007 are the projected construction of at least 3,000 classrooms and the recruitment and training of 7,000 new teachers each year. There are also plans to improve the curricula by incorporating the teaching of sciences and technology, entrepreneurship, and foreign languages, valuable skills that may be keys to better jobs. All instruction is given in French, and most textbooks come from France. As of 2006, 52 percent of the population over 15 is literate.

Children at the gate of a private school.

WILDLIFE APPRECIATION IN SCHOOLS

In 1987 the government of Madagascar asked the World Wildlife Fund (WWF) to help develop an environmental curriculum and produce teaching materials for the country's primary schools. Two years later, a series of educational posters aimed at developing behavior favorable to the conservation of nature was published. The poster series was called Ny Voaary, meaning "nature." Its success led to another sponsored publication, *Vintsy*, meaning "kingfisher," a bimonthly ecology magazine for secondary schools. Primary and secondary teachers still use these materials and are integrating environmental studies into the classroom. Schools lead the way in a crusade of tree planting and of broadcasting the dangers caused by cutting down the forests.

"None of the roads is as good as it looks on the map."

—*Maureen Ann Covell, in* Madagascar: Politics, Economics and Society

HEALTHY LIVING

Between 1975 and 1984 the government expanded the number of trained health-service workers from 3,900 to 8,200 as part of a policy aimed at putting a health facility within 6 miles (10 km) of every Malagasy family. The economy's poor performance unfortunately has caused cuts in this service. Today, though, 197 local health-care centers have been reinstated, but accessibility for most of the rural population remains poor—65 percent of rural people live more than 3 miles (5 km) away from a basic health-care center. Malnutrition is common in 65 percent of the citizens, and the population continues to increase in spite of a high infant mortality rate of 94 per 1,000 live births.

Parasitic diseases are hard to control because the irrigated rice fields and the streams that feed them often provide fertile breeding grounds for disease-carrying pests. Only 14 percent of rural residents have access to safe water as compared with 66 percent of urban dwellers who enjoy the same amenity. Diarrhea is thus rather common. Malaria is another great menace, infecting more than 1.2 million victims. So far more than 1 million mosquito nets for beds have been distributed to coastal areas and tourist spots for malarial prevention. Vaccinations for measles, supplements for vitamin A, and the treatment of diarrhea and malaria have increased at the community level. Nonetheless, hygiene is often lacking, with beaches and roadsides commonly used as bathrooms.

The small number of hospitals (the term here includes health centers) in the country provides on average one hospital bed for every 2,381 people. Most hospitals are in the towns, with some rural hospitals and clinics run by Christian missions. There are approximately 5,200 doctors, 410 dentists, and 175 pharmacists. Like Oman, a country on the southeast coast of the Arabian Peninsula, some 3 percent of the Malagasy national budget is spent on medical care (the United States spends about 16 percent of its national budget on health care). In Madagascar health insurance and other social benefits are available to the better-paid workers.

Bottles of medicine are available on the black market in urban areas, which are possibly sold by the families of patients who were given the medicine but never took it or died. International organizations such as the Médecins sans Frontières (Doctors without Borders) have made free medical care and follow-up available

Lack of proper sanitary facilities contributes to the spread of diseases and widely affects the quality of life.

to more than 2,500 street children. The organization has been working in Madagascar since 1987 and is currently engaged in projects to improve sanitary conditions.

In the countryside, Western medicine remains expensive and difficult to obtain. Many people still trust in traditional medicine that has been handed down through the generations. The rain forests are full of medicinal plants used in herbal treatments. The *raraha* (RA-rah) plant, for example, has anesthetic qualities and is used to ease sore gums and toothache. People in the countryside believe that illness may have more than a physical cause and that a healer does not cure the illness alone, but the whole person. The traditional healer is called the *ombiasy* (om-bi-ASH) and ministers by means of invocations or magic chanting, with perhaps an animal sacrifice and a pinch of herbs.

RELIGION

THE MALAGASY REGARD THEIR COUNTRY as the sacred land of their ancestors, who perpetually remain its rightful owners. Most of them believe in one God, in either the traditional or Christian sense. Many go to church, but that does not stop them from making sacrifices to their ancestors. Christianity is practiced hand in hand with traditional beliefs; it has not taken their place.

ORGANIZED RELIGION

The Christian faith has existed in Madagascar ever since King Radama I encouraged British missionaries to come there in the early 19th century. Over a period of 15 years they opened schools and chapels, produced the first dictionary of the Malagasy language, translated the Bible into Malagasy, and converted many to Christianity. The London Missionary Society introduced Protestant Christianity, but as French influence increased, so too did Roman Catholicism. The Protestant churches are found mainly in the highlands today, largely supported by the Merina people, while the more numerous Catholics are located mostly near the coast, where they enjoy support from the Betsileo people. Protestant and Catholic churches often compete for new adherents, and it is not unusual to find at least two churches in the central highland communities, one Protestant and one Roman Catholic, facing each other at opposite ends of the village.

Radama's widow was called the Wicked Queen and the Mad Queen of Madagascar. During her 33-year reign (1828–61), Queen Ranavallona prohibited Christian practices, killed those who disobeyed, and forced missionaries to leave. Churches built of stone in Antananarivo stand in remembrance of Madagascar's first Christian martyrs. One inscription

Above: **Missionaries run European-style ministries in a country where Christianity coexists with the cult of ancestor worship—both of which are widely practiced by many locals.**

Opposite: **The grand church of Betafo, located at a small town in Antsirabe.**

83

A church at Tôlañaro, formerly occupied by the French. Christian hymns are often sung in a distinctive Malagasy style.

reads, "Erected by the London Missionary Society in memory of 12 individuals who died in or near Madagascar in endeavoring to introduce on the island the blessings of civilization and the knowledge of the glorious gospel of the Blessed God."

About 41 percent of the population is Christian (24 percent Roman Catholic, 17 percent Protestant), and 7 percent Muslim. The majority of Muslims are found in Mahajanga, a breezy town on the northwest coast of Madagascar. Most are Comorian or Indo-Pakistani, while a small number are converted Malagasy. The rest of the population (52 percent) practice traditional beliefs.

TRADITIONAL WORSHIP AND DESTINY

The earliest Malagasy believed in a supreme being as well as secondary deities or spirits that inhabited waters, trees, and stones. They also respected creatures such as snakes, crocodiles, and lemurs, and held that humans have spirits that do not die after bodily death.

Even today, the people believe strongly in their ancestors' power to influence disasters (such as famine, drought, and cyclones), as well as happiness, prosperity, and luck. The dead are not regarded as having departed for good but are believed to remain with the family and play as important a role as they did when they were alive. Thus they must be honored, consulted, pleased, and asked to bestow good fortune on the family. A family may throw a party in honor of an ancestor. Each clan has its own beliefs, and practices different ways of burying their dead. An ancestor's soul can die if it is left out of the thoughts of its relatives.

THE BEGINNING OF MANKIND

This is the Malagasy version of how God put men on the earth. The god Andriananahary looked down from the heavens at a sunbaked, empty island. He wondered about the place. Could anyone survive there? Somebody would have to go and find out.

Andriananahary called to his son, Ataokoloinona, who was playing among the clouds. He explained the task: to go down to the earth and see what it was like. So Ataokoloinona floated down to the hot, dry land and looked around him. He was pleased to be given this mission and keen to return with a good report. But all around him was rock and sand. There were no plants, trees, or water, and the ground burned his feet. Sadly, he realized that he had to tell his father that nothing would be able to live on the earth.

So he tried to launch himself heavenward from the top of a sand dune, but something was very wrong. He could not fly. The sun was drying him up. In desperation, the boy dug a hole deep in the sand and hid himself. Night fell, and when there was no sign of his son, Andriananahary became worried. When sky and earth remained empty the next morning, he sent his servants to earth to search everywhere. They scurried in all directions but could find no trace of Ataokoloinona. Before long the heat began to affect them, too. The unhappy servants cracked and withered like dry leaves.

In pity, the god Andriananahary stretched out his hand, and there came thunder, lightning, and torrential rain. When the water reached the earth, the desert turned green and became a paradise, and the servants rejoiced. They stayed and became mortal men. But Andriananahary's son was never seen again. This well-loved legend helps to explain why the Malagasy consider that the ground itself is sacred and everything that grows in it is a gift from God.

At village gatherings people ask for their ancestors' permission to hold the meeting. Nobody is thought to be "dead and gone."

From such customs arise the idea of personal fate or destiny, called *vintana*, and the conviction that certain actions are *fady* (FAH-di), forbidden or taboo, because they bring bad luck. Belief in *vintana* is particularly strong in the coastal areas exposed to Islamic influence. They believe that there are certain times of high and low fortune, often foretold in the stars according to the moment of one's birth. So there are good or bad *vintana* periods. By choosing the "best times" for birth, circumcision, marriage, or burial, people can prevent accidents, illnesses, and trouble. The choice of a marriage partner is complicated by *vintana*. Every person is said to represent one of the basic elements of water, fire, wind, or hill. Wind cannot marry hill; fire can marry wind, but if fire marries water the fire will be put out.

Days of the week carry their own *vintana*. Monday is not a good day for work and can bring sorrow, but it is a good day for undertaking projects as they will last (such as building a house). Tuesday is an easy day, bad for important agreements but good for light work, travel, and having fun. Wednesday is "the day of poor return," so if one plants on that day, there will be a poor harvest and, even more alarming, if one goes traveling, one may not come back. This day is suitable to hold funerals. Thursday is the holiest day of the week, so no one can work in the fields on that day, but it is acceptable for most sacred rites except burial to be performed. Friday is a good day, set aside for enjoyment, but it is also the best day for funerals. Saturday (associated with nobility) is suitable for weddings and purification rites, and Sunday is God's day, when one

Steps up the sacred hill of Ambohimanga are lined with street vendors selling kebabs and other delicious food.

can work safely and succeed in the work undertaken. The village *ombiasy*, the healer and diviner, chooses suitable days for sowing, harvesting, marriage, and burial.

There are good times of day, too. Sunrise is usually a fortunate time to begin something, while the middle of the night is to be avoided.

The Malagasy believe strongly in luck. When something goes wrong, they believe they have offended an ancestor in some way. To the Malagasy, the *fady* rules and taboos are simply part of daily life, although the extent of the belief in *fady* and *vintana* varies from group to group and from one village to another.

Many other superstitions prevail as well. In Antananarivo, for example, people believe that evil spirits cannot climb steps, so buildings have many flights of steps to deter the harmful spirits. Almost everywhere in Madagascar people are sure that evil lurks at night, so homes are built without chimneys in case some spirit should enter there, and windows are shuttered and doors bolted securely after dark.

FUNERALS AND TOMBS

Reverence for one's ancestors means that one must give them an impressive farewell ceremony and a suitable dwelling place. Death is not normally a time for mourning. Without the blessing of the ancestors, nothing can go well. The Malagasy have a saying, "A house is for a lifetime; a tomb is for eternity." The word "dead" is not used; instead, the deceased has been "loosened" or "untied."

After a death, the family of the deceased immediately performs a ritual. They will go to a fast-flowing river with all their clothes and wash

A tomb carving in a human form illustrates the mix of tribal and Christian influences.

them, as well as the clothes they have on, to remove the contamination of death. They then attend to the deceased, washing the body and covering it with a white cloth. It is usually kept in the house for a few days while mourners gather. They will bring with them gifts of money that can only be used to pay for funeral expenses—it is *fady* to use it for any other purpose. A tribal elder's funeral may be a noisy affair that goes on all night, for some believe that they can banish death by wailing and drumming. The body is wrapped in an expensive shroud and buried, with the head facing east and the feet facing west, in whatever style is used in that area. In the west and on the plateau, children do not inherit their father's cattle. When he dies, his herd of cattle is slaughtered and their horns displayed on the tomb to show his importance.

The dead are always taken back to their ancestral tombs, even if they have spent much of their lives elsewhere or died away from their family land.

Not everyone is entitled to a burial. Among the Antaisaka people of Mananjary, twins were historically killed or abandoned in the forest after birth. Such an act is now against the law, but the superstition against twins still persists, and they may not be buried in a tomb. Sorcerers are dumped to the west of their village, their necks twisted so that they face south, and their bodies left in the open for wild animals to feed on.

All Malagasy names have meanings. When a person dies, relatives choose a new name for the deceased that highlights his or her good qualities—for example, "He who made work look easy" or "The woman who did her

FADY

Whether it is based on hope or fear, religion or superstition, the belief in *fady* rules most aspects of daily living. Such beliefs have endless variations. Customs or behavior forbidden in one place may be allowed in another only a few miles away. In one village, for example, it may be *fady* to eat pork, while a neighboring village is filled with squealing pigs.

Fady greatly affects the vital rice crop. Rice represents the toil of countless ancestors, and so it is holy. It may be *fady*, therefore, to move stones or building materials near the field because the noise might disturb the rice. It is also *fady* to sit in the doorway of a house while the rice is beginning to sprout, as it will impede the growth of the rice. Bad weather may also destroy the crop if anyone dares to gather marsh grass for matting at the time of planting.

It may be *fady* to sing while eating, or to whistle on a certain stretch of beach, or walk past a sacred tree. Feathers are *fady* for bedding or pillows because they symbolize flight, and thus might impede a stable and grounded home life. Instead, mattresses are stuffed with chopped straw. *Fady* also determines the direction in which one lies down to sleep. Men usually sleep with their heads to the north, which represents power, and their wives and children with their heads to the east, regarded as sacred. No one sleeps with feet to the east in case the person kicks the sunrise. In all things, ancestors must be respected. The prohibitions of *fady* are obeyed by tradition to prevent causing offense to anyone or anything and suffering bad luck and misfortune as a result. As *fady* differs from place to place, foreigners are generally exempted from observing them, but it is still advisable to be mindful to avoid offending the local people.

duty." Any living relative who has the same name as the deceased's newly acquired one must change his or her name, as it is *fady* to use the same name. The widow in mourning, according to Sakavala custom, dresses in old clothes and remains in the house. She does not speak to anyone except for close relatives. When the period of mourning (which can be several weeks) is over, she will dress in clean clothes, come out of the house, and speak to people to signify her return to the normal world.

Throughout the island, each tribe handles funerals and burial rites in its own way. The common factor is that all want their tombs to be more permanent than their houses. Those tombs might be in the shape of stone mausoleums, cave tombs, underground chambers with stone shelves, or walled enclosures that are painted. Other structures are sometimes used in place of tombs: long rows of stones with crosses mounted on them, carved wooden totem poles in the shape of people and animals, or obelisks marked only with a name (in which case the burial place is elsewhere, its location kept secret). The most elaborate tombs are those constructed by the Mahafaly people in the south, using intricately carved

This tomb sculpture featuring a carved airplane represents an ancient custom coupled with modern symbolism.

upright pillars that depict scenes from the person's life with sculptures and inscriptions. Sorrow belongs on the "cold" south side of a village, so tombs are usually sited there and built only at night. The shadow of a tomb must not touch the homes of the living.

TURNING OF THE BONES

Few customs are stranger than the one of *famadihana*. It is practiced mainly by the Merina and Betsileo people on the high plateau and is regarded as a duty that the living owe to the deceased. This involves opening the tomb, removing the old *lamba* that acted as a shroud, washing and rewrapping the body in a fine new silk shroud, and then replacing it reverently back in the tomb. Since the ancestors are not thought to have departed and their spirits are very much alive, they must be welcomed, talked to, and entertained. What is important is to show that they have not been forgotten, and family members may even hug them or dance with them. Tears and lamentation will not please the deceased.

The *famadihana* can last for up to a week, which means that the family will have to hire a band, employ an officiating *ombiasy*, sacrifice cattle, and pay for food and refreshments. Women who are trying to conceive may take small pieces of the old burial shroud. When put under their mattresses, these pieces of cloth are said to induce fertility. Even devout Christians may take part in the whole ritual. Depending on the family's wealth, the ceremony is held every third, fifth, or seventh year, but only during the dry season, between June and September.

Churches may frown on *famadihana* but have not attempted to forbid it because the custom is so deeply rooted in the lifestyle of the people. It is a principal source of their loyalty to their hometown or village, signifies their attachment to their tribal group, and demonstrates their respect for older people and the deceased. There are signs, however, that the practice is waning, partly because it is not in keeping with church custom, but mainly because of its cost.

LANGUAGE

MADAGASCAR'S LANGUAGE, MALAGASY, is almost as unique as its rare lemurs, chameleons, and orchids. Related to the Malayo-Polynesian family of languages spoken in the Malay Peninsula, with the addition of some words from Africa (Bantu languages and Kiswahili) and Arabia, Malagasy is a blend of Asia and Africa, with features not found anywhere else in the world.

GROWTH OF A LANGUAGE

In a country where the skills of reading and writing are still not universal, the spoken word remains highly important. The Malagasy language derived from Indonesia is remarkably uniform throughout the island. Although there are numerous regional variations, they are all linguistically related to the same Malagasy language.

The Antaimoro were the first people in Madagascar to adopt writing. Their holy men traveled widely throughout the country, adding an Islamic influence to the local language. Malagasy still uses Arabic-derived names for days of the week and months of the year. It also contains adopted words from English, French, and other tongues. As the first missionaries were British, Malagasy words relating to religion, education, or anything literary often have an English base, whereas anything to do with food or drink tends to be French-related, and words dealing with cattle and domestic animals come from the Kiswahili spoken in Africa.

The use of playful language is introduced in the early years, as children learn the symbolic importance of question-and-answer through the basic word game of riddling. Through learning to appreciate metaphor, they find that language is ambiguous. Here are some of their riddles:

Above: **A typical signboard found in Madagascar.**

Opposite: **A newspaper vendor displays her wares at her spot on a street in Antananarivo.**

"God's stick has water in its stomach" (sugarcane).

"Five men with round hats" (fingers).

"White chicks filling a hole" (teeth in mouth).

Wordplay is thus common in everyday talk and in Malagasy proverbs. For instance, "Darken the mouth of the cooking pot" is frequently used to describe dusk.

The mastery of unhurried speaking in public, called *kabary* (ka-BAHR), is still very much a part of Malagasy culture. Village elders can speak for hours, using witty double meanings, riddles, and complicated proverbs. It is a traditional skill, used especially at weddings and funerals. It is also widely used in daily talk, even if the younger folk do not have much time for it nowadays. The speakers delight in using more words than may be necessary. When asked how far away a particular place is, a Malagasy might answer, "A person walking fairly fast will probably reach there in the time it takes to cook a pot of rice."

A group of women in their colorful *lambas* chatting with each other.

WRITTEN RECORDS

In European literature, the earliest mention of Madagascar appears to have been made by Marco Polo in the 13th century. He wrote, "You must know that this island is one of the biggest and best in the whole world." He may have confused the island with Mogadishu in Somalia, however, because one of the spelling forms he used was Mogdaxo.

Other theories on the meaning of Madagascar are "Island of Ghosts" and "Island of Ancestors." Visiting Arabs called Madagascar "The Island

On the image: MAFONJA

TOMBOLA
SEKOLIN'NY MISIONA KATOLIKA ISOTRY
TIRAGE 8 JUILLET 1972
— DATE IRREVOCABLE —
VIDIN-KARATRA 50 FMG
GROS LOTS
RENAULT 4L   VELOMOTEUR

There are numerous dialects and local variations of Malagasy, but they are all mutually intelligible.

of the Moon." The Malagasy themselves use terms such as "The Great Island," "The Red Island," or "The Happy Island."

Among Marco Polo's mixture of reported truths and fictions was the mention of a giant bird that he called a gryphon and that the islanders called *rukhs* (ROOKS). A giant bird also appears in the Arabian Nights, where Sinbad the Sailor refers to a huge roc that can "truss elephants in its talons." Could this have been Madagascar's now-extinct elephant bird?

Radama I, who was given the title of "king" by Sir Robert Farquhar, British governor of Mauritius, sent out a request for missionaries to help with Madagascar's education and development. In 1817, two of those sent by the London Missionary Society were Welshmen David Jones and David Griffiths. With help from the king, they set about recording the Malagasy language in the European (Latin) alphabet. Phonetically, the language was almost perfectly consistent, with the consonants pronounced as in English and the vowels as in French. The first school was set up, and by 1835 the Bible was printed in Malagasy. Today it remains a language that is more spoken than written, very much a living language.

LANGUAGE DILEMMA

One problem often encountered in developing countries is whether to teach children in their mother tongue or a First World language. In 1972 Malagasy replaced French as the medium of instruction in schools in the hope of making education more accessible to all. But to be literate in a language used only on one island in the world does not help international communications. So in 1986 French was reintroduced in secondary schools. It is now the language of instruction in all schools and is used for literary, business, and administrative purposes. It is functional but not overpopular with the people; a qualified schoolteacher may teach in French and English, yet think in Malagasy.

Malagasy remains the spoken language throughout the island. English, which used to be spoken only to tourists, is now regarded as desirable for business transactions. To further cement the growing importance of the language, Madagascar has adopted English as its official third language. Among the many notices posted in Malagasy outside a church, which acts as a village's social center, there may be a flyer in French announcing the activities of the local "English Club," offering villagers the opportunity to learn to speak English "without hesitation" and become a "man of affairs or tourist guide." Madagascar also has one English-language newspaper, published by the English Speaking Union, called the *Madagascar News*. Newspapers like *L'Express*, *Les Nouvelles*, *Madagascar Tribune*, *Gazette de la Grande Ile* and *Midi Madagasikara* are mainly in French, as indicated by their names, but have columns in Malagasy.

In Antananarivo, French is spoken as often as Malagasy. In rural areas, however, it may be resented as a colonial language, so people use Malagasy at home, French in school, and English on the beer bottles—labeled Three Horses Beer, even though there are very few horses in Madagascar.

Since Madagascar gained its independence from France in 1960, many towns have reverted to their original names. Here are some of the old Malagasy and colonial French names:

Malagasy	**French**
Mahajanga	Majunga
Antsiranana	Diégo-Suarez
Nosy Boraha	Sainte Marie
Toamasina	Tamatave
Toliara	Tuléar
Tôlañaro	Fort Dauphin

Most people seem happy enough that the island itself is still called Madagascar, although in the Malagasy language it is Madagasikara.

Signboards advertising seaside hotels in French.

HOW TO SAY THE WORDS

The Malagasy alphabet has 21 letters. The following letters are not used: *c*, *q*, *u*, *w*, and *x*; *c* is replaced by *s* or *k*, and *x* with *ks*. The letter *o* is usually pronounced like *oo*, so *veloma*, meaning good-bye, is pronounced "ve-LOOM." The stress is usually on the penultimate syllable, although vowels that come at the end of a word are sometimes not pronounced at all. For example, *sifaka* is pronounced "SHE-fak." A general rule seems to be, "swallow as many syllables as you can and drop the last one." Sometimes the way one says a word changes its meaning—*tanana* (TAN-an-a) means "hand," but *tanána* (written with an accent and pronounced ta-NA-na) means "town." In general, though, the Malagasy language has no accents. Words with diacritics, or accent marks, are of French origin.

Malagasy is a poetic language. For example, the term for the early hours of the morning is translated "when the wild cat washes itself." Names of people and places also have meanings. Antananarivo, the capital, means "city of the thousand" because it is said that a thousand warriors originally guarded it. Words are often joined together (as in Welsh or German) to create long personal and place names. For example, people think nothing of pronouncing the name of the island's most famous king, Andrianampoinimerinandriantsimitoviaminandriampanjaka, without drawing a breath.

GREETINGS

Greeting a friend is a serious affair and must not be hurried. The traditional Malagasy greeting is to take an offered hand between one's own hands. Those who are more modern copy the French fashion, kissing three times on alternate cheeks, but they like to shake hands, too.

Salama (sal-AHM), a greeting in some coastal regions, is a variation of the Arabic *salaam*. The more common greeting is *manao ahoana* (mano OHN). Europeans are not called "white" because the color white is considered offensive; "white" refers to all that is ugly and of low quality, and an unreliable person is one who speaks "white words." So visitors are called *vazaha* (va-ZAH), or foreigner. The Malagasy are extremely courteous and do not speak loudly or shout. They do not speak lightly of old people or death.

Language and culture are reflective of the Malagasy's Indonesian origins, but there is also evidence of Afro-Arab settlers arriving in the coastal area before A.D. 1000.

SOME COMMON WORDS

Hello	*Manao ahoana* (mano OHN)
What news?	*Inona no vaovao?* (EE-nan vow-vow)
No news	*Tsy misy* (tsee MEESS)
Please/Excuse me	*Aza fady* (a-za FAAD)
Thank you	*Misaotra* (mis-OW-tr)
Good-bye	*Veloma* (ve-LOOM)

ARTS

THE MALAGASY ARE CLOSE TO NATURE. The artist, sculptor, wood-carver, or painter does not try to create an imitation of the world around him. His world is one in which a creator God has given the spirit of life to everything—humans, animals, plants, and stones alike. Even the deceased retain their spirit. So any work of art must be so beautiful that it pleases the spirit for whom it is intended and perhaps attracts the spirit to live in or feel associated with it. Even music is often something created out of emotion generated by a special moment.

For most poor people, an object's worth or beauty is judged by its usefulness. So weavers make cloth to wear or hats for shade; embroiderers make tablecloths or collars; and wood-carvers make tomb adornments in wood. Such tomb decorations acquire a sacred quality as well.

In the capital city of Antananarivo, there are museums of history, art, and archaeology, as well as the National Library. The Albert Camus Cultural Center is used for many concerts and film showings, while branches of the Alliance Française in Antananarivo and around the country stage cultural events. There is national pride in the country's cultural history. The restoration of the burned-down Queen's Palace in Antananarivo, for example, has drawn support from several provincial councils, notably those of Toliara and Toamasina, as well as that of the capital itself. There is also generous support from the German government.

Tsimbazaza Zoo includes displays of dinosaur bones and elephant bird eggs, and a terrarium of indigenous reptiles. The zoo also houses an ethnographic museum that showcases the cultures and peoples of the island.

Above: **Merina and Betsileo women are adept at French-style sewing and embroidery.**

Opposite: **An artisan presses fresh flowers into handmade paper. This ancient craft was practiced by the Antaimoro clan.**

LITERATURE

The most popular use of language in Madagascar is oral; there is a long tradition of oratory, known as *kabary* (ka-BAHR), that includes speech making and storytelling. Originating with the tribal councils of elders, this linguistic skill has been extended from political polemic to sheer entertainment. A masterful speaker spins a web around his subject, referring to it in clever metaphors and intricate proverbs and references, never coming directly to the point, to the delight of his audience. Such linguistic prowess is greatly admired.

Proverbs are rich and popular, combining wisdom and wit, as in the following examples.

"You can trap an ox by its horns and a man by his words."
"The man who refuses to buy a lid for the pot will eat badly cooked rice."
"If you are only a dung beetle, don't try to move mountains."
"Invite a big eater and he will finish the meal; advise a fool and he will waste your time."

Writing was first introduced to Madagascar by the Antaimoro people during the reign of King Andrianampoinimerina at the end of the 18th century. The Antaimoro people, who possibly came from the Arabian Peninsula, settled near the Matitane River in the southeast around the end of the 15th century. They were the only keepers of religious texts that contained writings known as Sorabé. Based on an Arabic script, they are filled with prayers, magic formulas, genealogies, memorable events, and legends. These texts were held in great awe, and the Antaimoro's ability to write also gave them power and prestige throughout the land.

Madagascar's well-established printing industry—introduced in the 1820s by the London Missionary Society—supports the production of written literature in Malagasy, including poetry, scholarly works, and contemporary writings, as well as the many newspapers.

LEGENDS

Legends are featured prominently in Madagascar's oral tradition. One of the many favorite tales is that of the *voronjaza* (voo-ROON-jahz) bird, or sickle-billed vanga.

The story is set in a time of raiding pirates and slave traders. A mother and her child took refuge in the thick forest. Raiders who were close by heard a baby crying and headed toward the sound, laughing cruelly and anticipating with delight what they would find. Then they heard the sound again, but at that moment the *voronjaza* hopped onto the branch of a tree and gave its call, which sounded just like the cry of a newborn baby. The pirates cursed the fact that they had been fooled by a bird and sailed away.

The mother, however, knew that the bird had saved her child's life, for the first wail from her baby had been real enough. So the *voronjaza* remains honored, and to this day it is *fady*, forbidden, to kill a *voronjaza*.

The Malagasy words were written on paper embedded with pressed dried flowers. The paper was made by using pulp from the *avoha* tree, and ink was extracted from the gum tree. The words were in an Arabic script so ancient that no one can decipher them today. This was the only form of writing in Madagascar until the first missionaries arrived. Unfortunately, the zealous considered the Sorabé books to be products of witchcraft and burned all that they could find.

There is scant famous Malagasy writing, perhaps due to the lack of diffusion, apart from the patriotic poetry of Jean-Joseph Rabearivelo, Jacques Rabemananjara, and Flavien Raniavo. Other poets known in Madagascar are Justin Rainizababololona, one of the first published Malagasy; Bruno Rahaingo, whose poems are politically engaged; and Ny Malodohasaha, whose writings coincided with the fall of the First Republic. The town of Fianarantsoa, an early center of learning, has gained a name as the island's contemporary literary capital. A number of writers have published their works there, among whom Emilson D. Andriamalala is probably the best known.

Moreover, there is a traditional style of love poetry perfected by the Merina called *hainteny* (HAY-ten-i). This can be soulful and profound, or somewhat more playful, as shown in this translation that is part of a series of questions with answers that have to be read between the lines.

"What will you say you love me like?"
"I love you like rice."
"Then you love me not, for you only keep it stored up for when you are hungry."

Books are extremely expensive in Madagascar. The country has few libraries and even fewer bookshops. In Antananarivo, popular bookstores include the Librairie de Madagascar and Espace Loisirs. The selection of English-language books outside of the capital is limited, as most books come from France. The French comic book stories of Asterix are available, alongside French novels and magazines. A few Christian books in Malagasy are printed on cheap paper by missionary societies.

Newspapers are a different matter. In Antananarivo alone, there are three daily newspapers all printed in red and black and sold by newsboys on the street to people on their way to work or at popular vendor stands. There is also the relatively new *Madagascar News*, printed in English.

MUSIC

Music is a part of most people's lives, although traditional styles and rhythms have often been invaded by Western pop music. The Malagasy, especially the men, like singing in harmony. Many of the songs are church hymns because Malagasy social life often centers around a church, but the singers love folk songs, too, sung in styles influenced by music from Polynesia to East Africa.

Local instruments include a cone-shaped drum of Indonesian origin and the *valiha* (va-LEE-a). This is similar to a zither, with 21 or more strings attached lengthways around a hollow bamboo tube. If the strings are attached to a rectangular sound box, it is called a *marovany* (MAH-ro-VAN). The instrument looks like a bassoon but is played like a harp to produce rippling chords. Expert players of the *valiha* include Tombo Daniel from Toamasina and Rakotozafy, who has recorded *valiha* music.

Many traditional instruments, made of bamboo or a gourd, produce only one note, such as the *kiloloka* (KEE-lo-LOOK) that whistles shrilly or the traditional Malagasy flute, the *sodina* (so-DEEN). Music is often made by a group of players producing harmonies and rhythmic variations as each musician contributes his single note. The most famous player of the *sodina* is Rakotofra.

The African cultural influence is evident in the many drums, rattles, and sounding animal horns commonly played. There are guitars and fiddles, too. The more contemporary popularity of the accordion reflects the recent French colonial era.

The best-known Malagasy musician is probably Paul Rahasimanana, called Rossy, who earned his fame by performing *vaky soava* (vahk SOOV), choral music with a strong beat accompanied by hand clapping. He added instrumental accompaniment and soon became popular, playing in concerts and on the radio. In the 1980s his band toured overseas. His most famous recording was *Island of Ghosts*, which seems a fitting theme for a place so bound up in its

The man on the right is carrying a gourd resonator with two sets of strings.

105

A man performs a traditional dance. The country's contact with many cultures has given it a rich legacy of artistic styles and forms of expression.

respect for the dead. In this piece of music, Rossy combined traditional styles with modern lyrics on the enduring themes of poverty, hope, and love. Rossy, together with other Malagasy artists, including D'Gary and Tovo, is also featured in the highly acclaimed music album *A World Out of Time*. The album was a result of their 1991 collaboration with American-born experimental guitarist Henry Kaiser. Two other volumes soon followed, with volume 2 being nominated for a Grammy award.

In the towns, posters invite local residents to jazz concerts—or to a spectacular fashion show that will attract men and women alike. The most successful local groups playing pop music in Malagasy style have been Mahaleo and Tarika Sammy (who made it to the international music world along with other artists like Jaojoby, Rajery, and accordionist Regis Gizavo). Other well-known contemporary pop groups and singers include Tearano, Freddy de Majunga, Tiana, Dama, and Rebika. There are occasional classical music concerts as well.

ARCHITECTURE

Building styles depend on the materials available. Brick and corrugated iron are used on the high plateau where there are hardly any trees left for timber. Coastal homes may have a framework of wooden poles, with walls and roof made of palm fronds, thatch, woven matting, or mud and wattle (interwoven reeds and thin poles). Where there is suitable wood, the Malagasy enjoy carving patterned posts or face-boards for verandas and porches.

The compass points of a house are important, and each direction has its own significance. For example, the north represents power and the south suggests bad influences. According to the Malagasy cosmological system, the north axis is superior to the south, and the east axis is superior to the west. Malagasy houses are always oriented on the north-south axis, as that is believed to correspond to the world of the living. Guests are to be seated in the north or northwest of the house, while the northeast corner is sacred to the ancestors, holding objects of ceremonial use. In the south part of the house may be the hearth, in a square pit, with cooking pots, ax, and firewood set against the wall. The east is considered sacred. The husband's bed is thus usually beside the east wall, where he sleeps with his head to the north.

Wood carvings are Madagascar's primary art form.

In the cities, houses are built mostly of red brick, but some blocks of plastered concrete are painted cream, green, or off-white. Antananarivo has some gracious buildings dating from French colonial days; these have tall windows, wrought-iron balconies, and shutters. Middle-income homes have two or three stories, often with the kitchen at the top, living quarters in the middle, and storage space below. Most town houses have wide balconies supported by brick columns and are crowned with steep, tiled roofs.

CRAFTS

There is an obvious distinction between articles made of recycled modern scrap and articles made of natural materials with a long tradition of design behind them, yet the Malagasy have become very ingenious at recycling castoffs. Discarded tomato puree cans are made into oil lamps, and soft drink cans become brightly colored model cars. Watering cans are made from milk-powder cans, and wire is used to create egg baskets or environmentally friendly mousetraps that catch the mouse alive, to be eaten or set free elsewhere. French-style, long-handled garden spades are made from bits of old cars. Discarded tires are turned into sandals. Raffia is woven into market baskets with leather handles or hats with wide brims. Rugs are made from raffia and rags.

True craftsmen carve in wood and horn. Wood carving from Ambositra is famous, as is the furniture made in Betsileo of valuable hardwoods. The objects created are most often practical and include headrests, stools, and walking sticks. Tourists buy boxes with inlaid designs, model sailboats, chess sets made from semiprecious stones, and solitaire, a one-player board game played with 32 pegs or counters. The goal is to jump over the pegs horizontally or vertically until there is only one peg left on the board. The beauty of almost anything in Madagascar is determined by its usefulness.

In the town of Antaimoro, a decorative papyrus-like paper, with dried flowers embedded in it, is used to make wall hangings and lampshades. It was originally produced from the pulped bark of the avoha tree, but now sisal is used as well.

Women enjoy wearing *lambas* made from locally produced cotton or silk colored with herbal dyes. The silk is woven from fibers produced by silkworms raised on mulberry or tapia leaves. Particularly attractive

A vendor sells beautifully woven straw hats.

SACRED ART

One of the more durable examples of "art" in Madagascar has a sacred application—tomb decorations in wood or stone. Mahafaly tombs (in the southwest) are among the most elaborately painted or decorated of any on the island. These may include scenes or details from the life of the deceased or more stylized geometric designs.

The people carve *aloalo* (a-LOOL), memorial posts sometimes 6–12 feet (2–4 m) high that are set up on the rectangular tomb or on the gravesite. The word *aloalo* means "shadow of death," and it was originally intended as a resting place for the deceased's soul, so the *aloalo* and grave area constitute a shrine.

In recent years, greater realism, and even an element of humor, has become evident in tomb decorations. The funerary art of the Sakalava (in the west) can be complex, with carved zebu cattle and fanciful birds. Sometimes the art incorporates male and female figures that appear surprisingly sexual to non-Malagasy eyes, but probably represent the notion of rebirth.

is the *lambahoany* (LAM-ba-OON), the colorful cloth of the widespread Sakalava group. Ornamental cloth is made of finely woven raffia, and decorative tablecloths and mats are crocheted or embroidered.

Market vendors do not have set prices for their goods, so all transactions involve a fair bit of bargaining. Much of the craftwork on sale is intended for tourists, but the Malagasy like to decorate their houses as well. A serious attempt is being made to stop the production and sale of items originating from endangered creatures, such as tortoise shell, snakeskin, coral, and stuffed lemurs.

TEXTILES

Weaving is popular in Madagascar and has distinct features not found anywhere else within the African context. Silk, cotton, wool, raffia, and bast fibers are used alone or in combinations on the many types of looms found on the island. Malagasy weaving technology appears to reflect the mixture of Malayo-Polynesian, African, and Arab influences that is also evident in the peoples' cultures. In Madagascar, only women weave.

The Merina loom, similar in style to those found in Southeast Asia, does not rely on a fixed structure of weight to create the required tension; instead, it uses the weight of the weaver's body.

Most cloth is woven in stripes of different widths and colors. It can have a border decorated with small silver beads. Silk weaving comes mostly from the Merina and Betsileo people; cotton, once widespread,

Brightly colored pottery for many uses on display at a street market.

is now mainly from Betsileo; wool is associated with the south; bast fiber with Merina, Tanala, and Betsileo; and raffia, the fiber most widely used, with Betsimisaraka, Sakalava, Merina, and Tanala.

The warp-striped *lamba* cloth used to be worn by everyone and removed only when some vigorous task had to be undertaken. Distinct from this common wrap is the *lamba mena*, the shroud reserved for wrapping dead bodies. The earliest records indicate that these were always woven of silk and dyed red. Now the color red is not always predominant and a shroud may contain colors prescribed by the *ombiasy*, who determines the most favorable colors for a particular ancestor.

IMPACT OF THE MODERN WORLD

In recent years, Madagascar's textile art has seen a revival of sorts with famous fashion houses such as Yves Saint Laurent using local handwoven fabrics in their creations. In Antananarivo, local fabrics dominate fashion runways. Increasingly, affluent Malagasy wear Western-inspired vests, ties, handbags, and hats made of these beautiful textiles.

Creative expression in the 21st century, such as film directing and photography, has arrived in Madagascar but is still very much in its infancy. The most renowned director is Raymond Rajaonarivelo, who studied cinema in France and has made films like *Quand Les Etoiles Rencontrent La Mer* (*When the Stars Meet the Sea*) and *Tabataba* (*The Spreading of Rumors*). The print media industry is well established; newspapers are popular and often critical of government policy. There is very little reading material available for children, however, apart from their schoolbooks.

Cotton *lambas* worn by both men and women often contain intricately designed patterns.

111

LEISURE

AS IN MANY OTHER COUNTRIES, Malagasy children seem always to be kicking a soccer ball around or playing a makeshift game of baseball or cricket in many districts across Madagascar. In schools, games such as soccer, volleyball, basketball, boxing, and tennis are primarily played as organized sports.

ENTHUSIASM FOR SPORTS

Athletics have become increasingly popular over the past two decades, and interregional school meets as well as professional participation in the All-Africa Games are common. Students

Above: **Young Malagasy people enjoy dancing at local clubs.**

Opposite: **Soccer is a very popular sport for many in Madagascar and is followed passionately.**

compete at soccer, too, using a local stadium in the mornings, with smartly dressed teams, uniformed referees, and linesmen. In the evenings and on the weekends, their fathers take over the stadiums for their games. Madagascar has a national soccer team nicknamed the Barea (named for a species of zebu that is also on the country's coat of arms), but the team has never qualified for the finals in the World Cup or the African Nations Cup tournaments. Newspapers keep readers up to date with news of local and world soccer stars. During the World Cup soccer seasons, many cafés display tablecloths featuring the top teams. Girls as well as boys play the game.

There is also enthusiasm for tennis, although it is an expensive sport to organize. Malagasy athletes excel in tennis, participating in both the Fed Cup (a competition in women's tennis) and the Davis Cup (a competition for men's tennis). Two sisters in particular, Dally and Natacha Randriantefy, have been outstanding in this sport, with Dally, who retired in 2006, winning

The Madagascar delegation parades during the opening ceremony of the 2006 Winter Olympic games in Turin, Italy.

Madagascar's first gold medal in the All-Africa Games in Harare in 1995. Cycling is popular, and tourists have discovered that the rough trails and country roads are ideal for scenic mountain biking. They also enjoy organized canoe trips on the rivers Tsiribihina and Manambaho in the west. Whale watching is fast gaining in popularity, especially around Maroantsetra and off the coast of Nosy Boraha. Tennis courts, swimming pools, and golf clubs in Antananarivo and some other major centers are legacies of French colonial occupation. A relatively new sport is horse racing, with interest and support from South Africa. Newspapers in Antananarivo carry details of handball league championships and table tennis competitions.

Madagascar first participated in the Olympic Games in 1964 and has sent outstanding athletes to subsequent Olympics, but has yet to take home any medals.

LOCAL SPORTS

If in the more traditional areas of Madagascar people seem to show little interest in organized Western-style sports, it does not mean they do not like to show off their athletic prowess and bravery. There are several indigenous sports events. In the highlands south of Antananarivo, in the cattle country of Ambositra, there is a form of bullfighting known as *tolon'omby* (to-lon-OMB) that resembles an American rodeo. Young men dash among bulls that are inside a stockade, trying to catch one by the horns (or hump or tail) and hold on as long as possible. The crowd roars its approval at displays of bravery and skill or jeers if the youth falls too quickly.

The Sakalava have a style of martial arts called *moraingy* (mor-AIN-gi) where two opponents swing blows at each other with arms and bare fists until one steps back. The fighting is fast and tough, with emphasis on agility. The objective is to knock one's opponent flat on his back.

As might be expected from a population closely linked to Indonesia and the East, oriental martial arts are popular, although there are uneasy memories of the 1985 street violence in Antananarivo attributed to the kung fu clubs there.

LIVING IT UP

The board game *fanorona* (fan-or-OON), a complicated Malagasy version of checkers, is a national pastime. A complex grid of crisscrossed lines is marked out on the ground (or on specially made stone blocks in public arcades) and two opponents move counters, encouraged by a crowd. Each player tries to "eat" his opponent's pieces. It is a leisurely game that does not require speed, for there are traps everywhere. The philosophy of *fanorona* rests in the idea that life presents many possibilities. The outcome

YOUTH ORGANIZATIONS

There are three Scout organizations—the Scouts of Madagascar, the Unionist Scouts of Madagascar, and the Catholic Boy Scout Association of Madagascar—with an overall membership of about 9,473 boys and girls. All three focus their main efforts toward community development, taking an active part in rural education and helping with instruction in adult literacy classes. The Scouts also have helped during national disasters, undertaking relief projects, rescuing farmers during floods, and rounding up cattle to move them to higher ground. Some churches sponsor youth clubs, and the church often acts as the social center for the community.

prized most by experienced players is a tie or becoming deadlocked, for the goal is not direct aggression but to stop one's opponent from moving. There is even a national *fanorona* organization.

Another game is *katra* (KAH-trr), a mancala game that involves shifting piles of stones around a board until one player has won all the stones.

The café version of football, foosball, with rows of wooden players on little metal rods, is highly popular with young men. They play pool or table tennis as well. The departure lounge of a small-town airport is sometimes used as a social club in the evenings. Men gather there for a beer or to play cards or dominoes.

Young children play hopscotch, scratching an eight-square pattern in the dust and hopping on one foot, while kicking a piece of wood onto the next square. Older kids listen to imported music on cassettes or twist happily at the local dance clubs. Antananarivo has about a dozen dance clubs, and most towns have at least one.

POPULAR MEDIA

The government-controlled Malagasy Broadcasting System broadcasts television as well as radio programs in Malagasy and French. On most days television viewing starts at noon and includes cartoons, sports programs, news in French and Malagasy, and films from France and the United States. Not many homes have television—only 25 out of 1,000 households own television sets—which is one set in every 40 families.

There are few movie theaters apart from those in Antananarivo and the larger towns. In the capital city, the Albert Camus Cultural Center has theater programs and concerts, varying from classical to jazz and rock. Films are shown at the Alliance Française centers (found in many towns) and at several embassies in Antananarivo.

Young Malagasy people enjoying a game of basketball.

FESTIVALS

ALTHOUGH THERE ARE RELIGIOUS AND POLITICAL festivals developed from colonial influence and contact with the Western world, old cultural festivals connected with the natural cycles of the year are also celebrated in Madagascar. In some places, for example, a Festival of Trees or Festival of Rice is held in April or May to celebrate the harvest.

This appeals to people in the rural areas, where the preparation, growth, and harvesting of rice mark the progress of time far more memorably than any public holiday. A successful rice harvest ensures survival, so it is hardly surprising that common expressions concerning time refer to how long it takes to cook a pot of rice or the time it takes for rice seedlings to sprout.

Other holidays mark religious or political events. If a holiday falls on a Thursday, it is extended to Friday to create a longer weekend.

The Catholic and Protestant churches observe religious festivals with worship services in much the same way as anywhere else in the world. The Malagasy have adopted from the French Catholics their love of incense, processions, and ceremonial rituals. They observe Christmas and Easter, the main Christian festivals, in conventional style. Father Christmas is known as le Bonhomme Noël in French or Dadabenoely in Malagasy and is portrayed in the usual red outfit trimmed with white fur despite the heat of a tropical summer in December. The small Muslim minority celebrates Eid ul Fitr (or Eid al-Fitr) to mark the end of the month of fasting during Ramadan. Gifts will be given to children who fast for the first time or have completed their entire month of fasting.

Above: **Winnowing rice calls for patient hands. The government encourages the blending of old and new cultural expressions. The celebration of the rice harvest in the Festival of Rice is one of the seasonal festivals introduced in recent times.**

Opposite: **A Malagasy trio plays folk music during the Festival of Rice.**

119

"Ry tanindraza nay malala ô!"— "Oh, Our Beloved Fatherland!"—the national anthem of Madagascar.

POLITICAL HOLIDAYS

On March 29 (Insurrection Day) people remember the 1947 rebellion led by Joseph Raseta and Joseph Ravoahangy against French domination. The insurrection was crushed and thousands of Malagasy were killed: some estimates say as many as 80,000 perished. Nevertheless, it was the beginning of a popular movement that eventually led to the country's longed-for independence in 1960.

This event is celebrated as Independence Day on June 26. There is a weeklong program of patriotic events leading to the day, when schoolchildren parade with banners proclaiming the republic's motto, "Fatherland, Liberty, Progress." They sing the national anthem and watch the national flag being raised. Speeches, singing, and processions follow, and there is usually a Grand Ball and family feasting in the evening.

OFFICIAL PUBLIC HOLIDAYS

January 1	New Year's Day
March 29	Insurrection Day
April*	Good Friday, Easter Sunday and Monday
May 1	Workers' Day (Labor Day)
May 25	Organization of African Unity Day
May*	Ascension Day
May*	Pentecost Monday
June 26	Independence Day
August 15	Assumption Day
November 1	All Saints' Day
December 25	Christmas Day
December 30	Republic Day, or Anniversary of the Democratic Republic of Madagascar

* The exact dates vary from year to year.

The Anniversary of the Democratic Republic of Madagascar (or Republic Day) is recognized in similar style on December 30.

The internationally observed Labor Day on May 1 was instituted when Communist ideals were being copied during the presidency of Didier Ratsiraka, but it is now observed as Workers' Day by the present trade unions.

Madagascar is a member of the African Union (AU) and a member of the United Nations, so May 25, which is the Organization of African Unity Day, is an opportunity to spotlight the country's political links with the African mainland. The Malagasy do not consider themselves to be Africans, but because of the legacy of French colonial rule, the island has developed political, economic, and cultural ties to the French-speaking countries of western Africa. It is also regarded as advantageous to have friendly trade links with the mainland.

TRADITIONAL FESTIVITIES

The New Year is Madagascar's most popular festival and a time for gift giving. Also celebrated is Alahamady Be, or the first new moon in the first month of the Malagasy New Year.

The *famadihana* ceremony of reburial should be undertaken every year for one or more ancestors, but few families can afford this. By law, this ritual must take place between June and September, presumably because they are the cooler months and the opening of a tomb will present less of a health hazard in terms of unpleasant odors and disease.

Malagasy guards parading during an Independence Day celebration. Processions, parades, and feasting accompany the festivities and special events observed by the people.

121

Two generations of royal descendants attending a New Year's festival held in Ambohimanga.

Circumcision is practiced in Madagascar as a fertility rite. It is performed on boys generally between 5 and 6 years old, also mostly during June to September, as these dry, cool months help in the healing of the wound from circumcision. Circumcision is not regarded as the rite of passage between adolescence and adulthood as it is in many parts of the African mainland. Among the Antaimoro people in the southeast the ceremony is observed only once every seven years and the feast may go on for several days. There are specific *fady* rules: uncircumcised boys are not

MUSIC FESTIVAL

Donia is a traditional music festival held at Nosy Be in the month of May or June. Scores of musicians from parts of Madagascar, Mauritius, Réunion, and Seychelles enliven this four-day annual event. In November or December, Antananarivo hosts a contemporary music festival. Madajazzcar, a jazz festival, is usually held in October or November.

THE MALAGASY CALENDAR

In traditional Malagasy culture, time and place come together in the home. Even without conventional education, country folk can count the passing of the lunar months by noting the four walls and corners of their houses in relation to their known compass points. That, supposedly, is why there are no round huts in Madagascar as there are in Africa. The year starts with Alahamady, meaning New Year, in the northeast. The succeeding months each reveal differing predictions of *vintana*, or fortune, according to the phase of the moon.

"men" and may not marry, nor be laid in the family tomb. While still uncircumcised, boys must not handle sharp iron instruments

Another celebrated occasion is when a baby's hair is cut for the first time. Among the Antambahoka in the south, the baby's grandparents will do the honor of cutting the hair. For the Merina people, only a man whose parents are still alive is allowed to perform the ritual. The baby is then put in a basin filled with water and bathed. Afterward, the family will have a meal of rice, zebu meat, milk, and honey.

Happy children in a west coast primary school. Circumcision is commonly performed on boys before they reach the age of ten.

FOOD

MADAGASCAR'S CULINARY TRADITIONS ARE just as unique as its people. Cuisines of French, Chinese, Indian, and to a lesser degree, East African and Arabian cultures are reflected in many Malagasy dishes. Malagasy cook French-influenced beef, chicken, and seafood cuisine exquisitely for their European residents or foreign visitors. For themselves, they insist on having rice at nearly all of their meals.

Most Malagasy serve their meals on a mat on the floor. All the food is laid out at the same time, and large spoons are used to scoop food from common dishes. Tradition requires that the oldest member of the family eats and drinks first but should always stop eating before the young are served to make sure there will be enough food for them.

RICE

The Malagasy eat about a pound (half a kilogram) of rice, which they call *vary* (VAR), daily and consider themselves poorly treated if it is not available. For variety, they cook it differently for each meal. At breakfast, the rice may be watery (like a rice porridge), or eaten dry and sprinkled with sugar or with any available sliced fruit. For lunch and supper, it is eaten dry and served with onion or another vegetable. In well-to-do households, French bread spread with butter replaces rice as breakfast food. Occasionally, sugar or sweetened condensed milk is taken with the bread.

A Malagasy cook does not decide whether or not to have rice but merely chooses what to have with it, using what is locally available and in season. Everything goes with rice—perhaps a boiled or fried egg, or

Above: **A vendor selling palm marrow, which can be eaten raw, as in a salad.**

Opposite: **Local produce being sold at a market in Madagascar makes a brillant splash of color.**

a few bits of stewed or boiled zebu beef, fish, chicken, or duck. Popular side dishes to go with rice are peas flavored with pork, whitefish with zucchini and tomato, beans in tomato sauce, and pumpkin-peanut puree. With this may come a small bowl of *ranovola* (RAHN-o-VOOL), which is water boiled with the residue in the rice pot, or *brêdes* (BREED), which is boiled greens, to finish off the meal.

Rice is not only a substantial staple food, it is also a prominent feature of Malagasy culture. Growing rice requires more people than one household can provide, so families have to be friends with each other. They join together to trample the ground to prepare it for the planting of seeds, take turns in "rice watching"—making sure that the birds do not eat the sown seed and that cattle or wild pigs do not trample the young plants—and then harvest the crop. Even pounding the rice with a heavy wooden pestle can be turned into a sort of dancing game in which a circle of four to six women throw the pestle across to one another while keeping up a steady rhythm.

FAVORITE FOODS

The national meat dish is *romazava* (room-a-ZAHV), a beef and vegetable stew in thin gravy with tomato, onion, and a hint of ginger. It is served with rice, spinachlike greens, and perhaps a salad. Another favorite is *ravitoto* (RAH-vee-TOOT-o), which is made of shredded cassava leaves with peanuts or fried pork. Red meats such as beef are a luxury, so small mammals often end up in the cooking pot. One local official remarked sadly, "Soon, all the lemurs will be extinct because they are so tasty." Villagers usually eat beef only occasionally, perhaps after a rare ceremonial slaughter of one of their precious zebu.

Their cooking is seldom strongly spiced; instead, commonly used ingredients like garlic, onion, ginger, tomato, mild curry, and salt are used to flavor their dishes. In the coastal areas, the use of coconut milk, vanilla, and spices such as cloves are popular. The Malagasy also enjoy mouth-searing sauces, though, such as the Indian-style condiment made of pickled mango, lemon, and other fruits. Usually eaten along the coast, this condiment is growing in popularity among many Malagasy highlanders. Other hot sauces include a fiery pepper sauce, and *rougaille* (roo-GUY), made from tomatoes, ginger, onions, lemon, and hot peppers.

They bake their bread, *mofo* (MOOF), in long thin loaves like French baguettes. In many villages, cassava or manioc root (which looks like a yam but has its own taste) is used as a bread substitute.

Chicken is on the menu in many variations and so is turkey, a bird not restricted by any local *fady*. Only gray-haired people may raise, though not eat, geese, since they have the gray hair that dispels the *fady* of the gray geese. Coastal fishers add crab, crayfish, shrimp, prawns, oysters, and many varieties of fish to their menu, although most of the catch is sold to hotels and restaurants rather than eaten at home.

Drying stacks of fish around a fire. Fish is easily caught on the island and is commonly used in many local Malagasy dishes.

EATING OUT

Going to a restaurant is an indulgence for the rich only. A lunchtime excursion is not as popular as an evening one because of the midday heat. In the evening, after a drink perhaps on an open veranda, dinner may last from 7 p.m. until late at night. The menu might include paella, a mound of seasoned rice surrounded by shrimp, pieces of chicken, hunks of crab, and lobster claws with a tomato, onion, and shrimp sauce. Vegetarian dishes are limited in many areas of Madagascar, and bean dishes are not as common as in mainland Africa. Some Indian restaurants

A vendor selling fresh local fruits in a market.

in Antananarivo and Mahajanga, however, do serve vegetarian food.

The influence of their ancestral lands is found in the popularity of Chinese and Indian restaurants. They have adapted the noodle-rich Chinese soup into a most filling meal, with greens and bits of seafood or chicken in a broth prepared with coriander and served with a sprinkling of soy sauce.

Those who prefer a less expensive meal will find fast-food sellers on street corners, where rows of vendors offer snacks in abundance. Most common is *mofo gasy* (MOOF gash), Malagasy bread made from a batter of sweetened rice flour and cooked over greased circular molds. This is a popular breakfast item, often enjoyed with a cup of coffee. There are many varieties of bread, one of which is made with chopped greens, tomatoes, and peppers. Other street snacks include deep-fried corn-flour donuts, rice pudding, and homemade yogurt. There are also curious relics of French colonial occupation in the form of tearooms selling sandwiches, sausage rolls, ice cream, cakes, and pastries.

SATISFYING A SWEET TOOTH

Dessert in Madagascar is usually fruit. From October to December there are fresh pineapples, lychees, strawberries, mangoes, guavas, and bananas growing wild that can be picked and eaten on the spot. In the markets, oranges, peaches, pears, apricots, and apples are available. Coconut is eaten in fresh slices, drunk (as water from the nut), or cooked with brown toffee (caramel) into sweets. The Malagasy serve bananas in many ways: fried in batter, cooked inside a pancake, or flamed in rum, which can be considered the national dessert. Nibblers buy slices of *parique* (pa-REEK), made from peanuts, rice, and sugar, and wrapped and baked in banana leaves. There is a local dark chocolate with a bitter flavor, and peanut brittle or loose peanuts are always available.

Malagasy cheeses are made almost exclusively in the south central highlands, including a delicious pepper cheese. Zebu cattle provide little milk, so there are few other dairy products.

DRINKS

Although the poor have no choice, the water that comes out of the communal taps is seldom safe to drink by Western standards. The common beverage is *ranovola*, rice water, which is water boiled in an almost-empty rice pot, flavored by leftover grains of burned rice (boiling makes it safer to drink than water from the tap or river). It is strained and served cold. Fresh milk is not easily available, so the Malagasy drink their coffee or tea without milk, providing sticky condensed milk for the strange foreigners who seem to require it.

Coconut milk, made from the white meat of the coconut, is a popular drink in the coastal towns: mixed with rum it becomes *punch aux cocos* (PAHN-ch aw KO-ko). There are several varieties of commercially distilled rum, often with added vanilla, honey, or lemongrass flavors. Variations of crude alcohol made from rice, sugarcane, coconut, or lychees are made for local consumption. The national beer is a lager named Three Horses, and there are two stronger brews called Gold and Queen's.

Small vineyards, mostly around Ambalavao and Fianarantsoa, produce fruity local wines such as Domremy, d'Antsirabe, Betsileo, and Côte de Fianer that come as red, white, rosé, and gris (a dry-tasting, pinkish wine).

ROMAZAVA (MEAT AND VEGETABLE STEW)

2 teaspoons (10 ml) peanut or vegetable oil
1 pound (0.5 kg) beef, cubed
1 pound (0.5 kg) pork shoulder, cubed
2 or 3 boneless and skinless chicken breasts, cut into bite-size pieces
6 medium tomatoes, chopped
1 medium onion, chopped
7 garlic cloves, chopped
2 inches (5 cm) fresh ginger, peeled and cut into thin strips
1/2 pound (0.25 kg) spinach, roughly shredded
Salt and pepper to taste
Optional: 1 green pepper and 1 stalk of celery, both chopped

Heat the oil in a heavy saucepan and sear the beef lightly, without browning. Add water to cover the beef. With the lid on the saucepan, let the water come to a boil over high heat. Lower the flame and simmer the beef for 25 to 30 minutes. Add the pork and simmer for another 30 minutes. The chicken may then be added and allowed to stew for 10 minutes. Add the tomatoes next and continue cooking. Once the tomatoes have been cooked into a sauce, add the onion, green pepper and celery, if using, garlic, and ginger and cook for 10 minutes more. Last, add the spinach and the salt and pepper to taste. Stir until the spinach wilts; remove the saucepan from the heat. Serve the stew hot with white rice. This recipe makes six to eight servings.

SALADY VOANKAZO (FRUIT COMPOTE WITH LYCHEES)

1 cup (230 g) pineapple, diced
1 cup (230 g) cantaloupe, diced
1 cup (230 g) oranges, thinly sliced
1/2 cup (115 g) strawberries, sliced
1/2 cup (115 g) canned lychees (or fresh if available)
1/2 cup (115 g) sugar
1/2 cup (115 g) water
1/4 teaspoon (dash) salt
2 tablespoons (30 ml) lemon juice
2 tablespoons (30 ml) pure vanilla extract

Combine the pineapple, cantaloupe, oranges, and strawberries in a big bowl and mix well. Scatter the lychees over the top of the fruit, and set the bowl aside. In a saucepan, combine the sugar, water, salt, and lemon juice, and bring the mixture to a boil over a high flame. Let thicken slightly for about a minute; stir in the vanilla extract. Pour the hot syrup over the fruit, then chill the bowl of fruit in the refrigerator for about an hour. Scoop the fruit into individual glasses or bowls and sprinkle a drop or two of vanilla extract over each portion before serving. This recipe is sufficient for six portions.

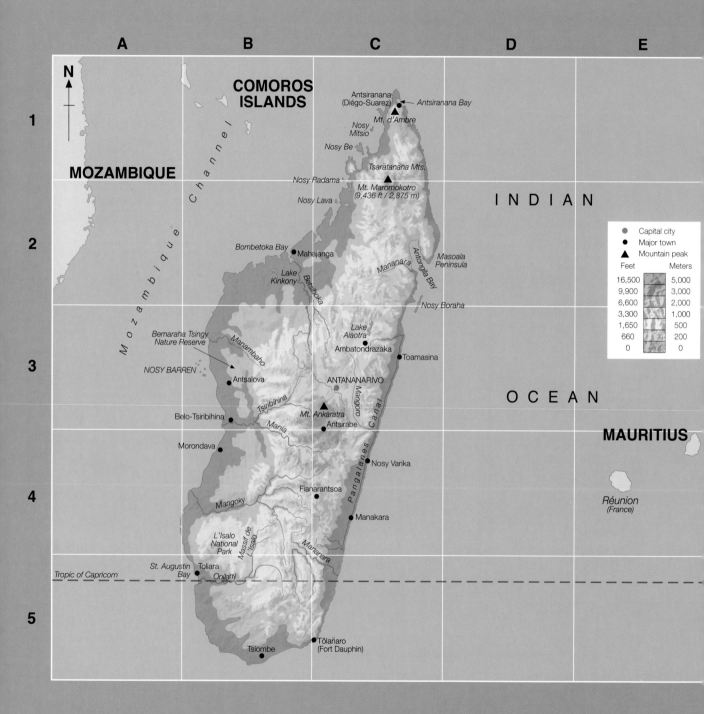

N

COMOROS ISLANDS

MOZAMBIQUE

Antsiranana
(Diégo-Suarez) ● ◄── *Antsiranana Bay*
▲
Mt. d'Ambre

Nosy Mitsio

Nosy Be

Tsarätanana Mts.

Nosy Radama
Mt. Maromokotro
(9,436 ft / 2,875 m)

I N D I A N

Nosy Lava

Mozambique Channel

Bombetoka Bay ● Mahajanga

Masoala Peninsula

Lake Kinkony

Betsiboka

Mananara

Antongila Bay

Nosy Boraha

Bemaraha Tsingy Nature Reserve

Manambaho

Lake Alaotra

NOSY BARREN
● Ambatondrazaka

ANTANANARIVO ●
● Toamasina

● Antsalova

Tsiribihina

Mangoro

O C E A N

Mania
Belo-Tsiribihina ●
▲
Mt. Ankaratra
● Antsirabe

Canal

Pangalanes

MAURITIUS

Morondava ●

● Nosy Varika

Mangoky

Fianarantsoa ●

Réunion
(France)

● Manakara

L'Isalo National Park

Massif de L'Isalo

Mananara

St. Augustin Bay Toliara
Tropic of Capricorn ● Onilahy

Tsiombe ● ● Tôlañaro
(Fort Dauphin)

● Capital city
● Major town
▲ Mountain peak

Feet		Meters
16,500		5,000
9,900		3,000
6,600		2,000
3,300		1,000
1,650		500
660		200
0		0

MAP OF MADAGSCAR

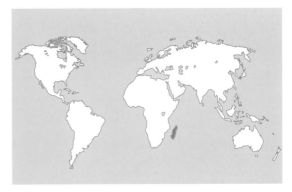

ECONOMIC MADAGASCAR

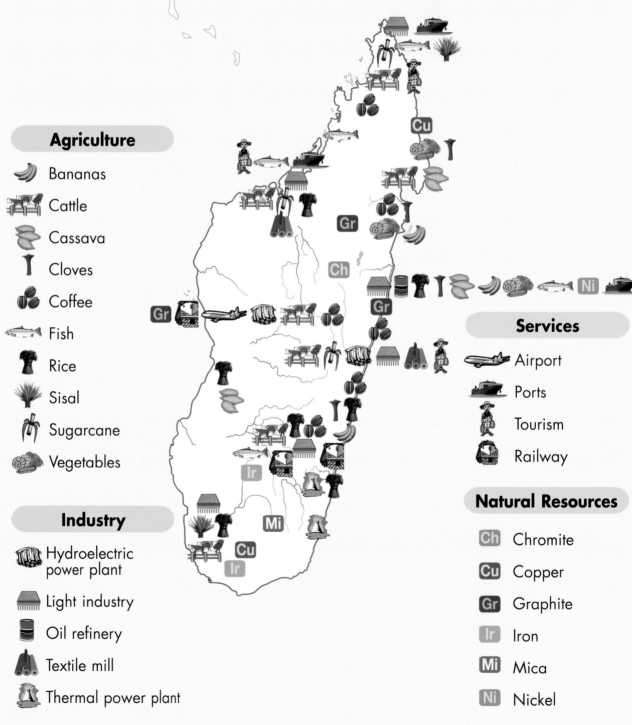

Agriculture

- Bananas
- Cattle
- Cassava
- Cloves
- Coffee
- Fish
- Rice
- Sisal
- Sugarcane
- Vegetables

Industry

- Hydroelectric power plant
- Light industry
- Oil refinery
- Textile mill
- Thermal power plant

Services

- Airport
- Ports
- Tourism
- Railway

Natural Resources

- Ch Chromite
- Cu Copper
- Gr Graphite
- Ir Iron
- Mi Mica
- Ni Nickel

ABOUT THE ECONOMY

OVERVIEW

Madagascar's positive economic outlook in recent years is due largely to its large-scale structural reforms that include privatization and liberalization of its economy. Foreign investors are aggressively courted and given tax breaks. Agriculture, fishing, and forestry, however, still make up the core of the economy, employing 80 percent of the population and contributing to more than one-fourth of the country's GDP.

GROSS DOMESTIC PRODUCT (GDP)

US$17.27 billion (2006 estimate)

GDP GROWTH RATE

4.7 percent (2006 estimate)

INFLATION RATE

12 percent (2006 estimate)

WORKFORCE

7.3 million

UNEMPLOYMENT RATE

5.9 percent

CURRENCY

1 Malagasy ariary (MGA) = 5 iraimbilanja
Notes: 10,000; 5,000; 1,000; 500; 200; 100 MGA
Coins: 50; 20; 10; 5; 4; 2; 1 ariary; 2; 1 iraimbilanja
1 USD = 1,823 MGA (August 2007)

NATURAL RESOURCES

Graphite, chromite, coal, bauxite, salt, quartz, tar sands, semiprecious stones, mica, fish, hydropower

AGRICULTURAL PRODUCTS

Coffee, vanilla, sugarcane, cloves, cocoa, rice, cassava, beans, bananas, peanuts, livestock products

INDUSTRIES

Meat processing, seafood, soap, breweries, tanneries, sugar, textiles, glassware, cement, automobile assembly plant, paper, petroleum, tourism

MAJOR EXPORTS

Coffee, vanilla, shellfish, sugar, cotton cloth, chromite, and petroleum products

MAJOR IMPORTS

Capital goods (production equipment like machinery that is used to produce other goods), petroleum, foodstuffs, consumer goods (goods for personal use such as food, medicine, and clothing)

MAJOR EXPORT PARTNERS

France 31.6 percent, United States 31 percent, Germany 8.8 percent (2005)

MAJOR IMPORT PARTNERS

France 16.8 percent, China 10.7 percent, Iran 8 percent, Mauritius 6.7 percent, Hong Kong 5 percent, South Africa 4.9 percent (2005)

LAND USE

Arable land: 5.03 percent; permanent crops: 1.02 percent; others (including grassland and wooded areas): 93.95 percent (2005 estimates)

CULTURAL MADAGASCAR

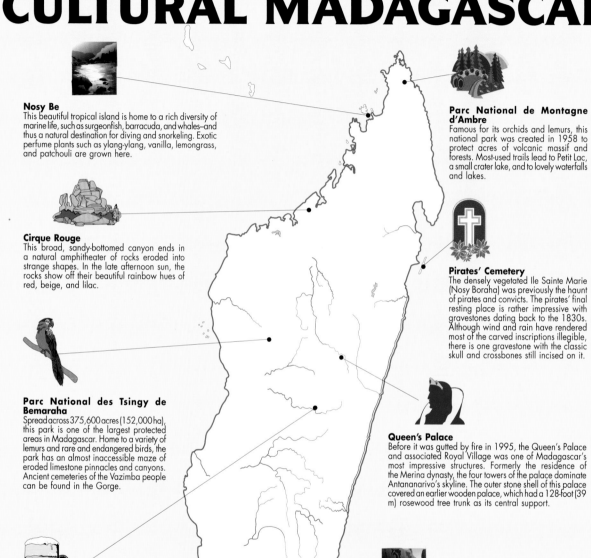

Nosy Be

This beautiful tropical island is home to a rich diversity of marine life, such as surgeonfish, barracuda, and whales—and thus a natural destination for diving and snorkeling. Exotic perfume plants such as ylang-ylang, vanilla, lemongrass, and patchouli are grown here.

Cirque Rouge

This broad, sandy-bottomed canyon ends in a natural amphitheater of rocks eroded into strange shapes. In the late afternoon sun, the rocks show off their beautiful rainbow hues of red, beige, and lilac.

Parc National des Tsingy de Bemaraha

Spread across 375,600 acres (152,000 ha), this park is one of the largest protected areas in Madagascar. Home to a variety of lemurs and rare and endangered birds, the park has an almost inaccessible maze of eroded limestone pinnacles and canyons. Ancient cemeteries of the Vazimba people can be found in the Gorge.

Antsirabe

This town south of Antananarivo was founded in 1872 by Norwegian missionaries as a health retreat. Although the thermal baths are no longer maintained, the town's mineral-rich water was traditionally believed to cure ailments like rheumatism and liver and gallbladder problems. Antsirabe is also known for its beer and *pousse-pousse* (passenger cart similar to the Chinese rickshaw).

Parc National de Montagne d'Ambre

Famous for its orchids and lemurs, this national park was created in 1958 to protect acres of volcanic massif and forests. Most-used trails lead to Petit Lac, a small crater lake, and to lovely waterfalls and lakes.

Pirates' Cemetery

The densely vegetated Ile Sainte Marie (Nosy Boraha) was previously the haunt of pirates and convicts. The pirates' final resting place is rather impressive with gravestones dating back to the 1830s. Although wind and rain have rendered most of the carved inscriptions illegible, there is one gravestone with the classic skull and crossbones still incised on it.

Queen's Palace

Before it was gutted by fire in 1995, the Queen's Palace and associated Royal Village was one of Madagascar's most impressive structures. Formerly the residence of the Merina dynasty, the four towers of the palace dominate Antananarivo's skyline. The outer stone shell of this palace covered an earlier wooden palace, which had a 128-foot (39 m) rosewood tree trunk as its central support.

Réserve Privée de Berenty

World famous, this reserve is enclosed by spiny desert, sisal plantations, and the Mandrare River. The reserve contains nearly one-third of the remaining tamarind gallery forest in Madagascar, and about 500 ring-tailed lemurs and numerous sifaka lemurs abound. Birdwatching is also popular, with nearly 100 bird species to look out for.

ABOUT THE CULTURE

OFFICIAL NAME
Repoblikan'i Madagasikara (Republic of Madagascar)

FLAG DESCRIPTION
Two equal horizontal bands of red (top half) and green with a vertical white band of the same width on the hoist side.

TOTAL AREA
226,657 square miles (587,042 square km); land: 224,533 square miles (581,540 square km); water: 2,124 square miles (5,500 square km)

CAPITAL
Antananarivo

ETHNIC GROUPS
Malayo-Indonesian (Merina and related Betsileo) 39.7 percent, Côtiers (Betsimisaraka, Tsimihety, Antaisaka, Sakalava) 24.5 percent, French 6 percent, Creole 4 percent, Indian 3 percent, Chinese 2 percent, Comorian 1 percent

RELIGIOUS GROUPS
Indigenous beliefs 52 percent, Christian 41 percent, Muslim 7 percent

BIRTHRATE
38.6 births/1,000 population (2007 estimate)

DEATH RATE
8.51 deaths/1,000 population (2007 estimate)

MAIN LANGUAGES
Malagasy (official national language), French (official language), English (official language)

LITERACY
52 percent (for those aged 15 and above) (2006)

NATIONAL HOLIDAYS
New Year's Day (January 1), Insurrection Day (March 29), Good Friday (date varies), Easter Sunday (date varies), Easter Monday (date varies), Labor Day/ Workers' Day (May 1), Organization of African Unity Day (May 25), Ascension Day (date varies), Pentecost Monday (date varies), Independence Day (June 26), Assumption Day (August 15), All Saints' Day (November 1), Christmas Day (December 25), Republic Day (December 30)

LEADERS IN POLITICS
Philibert Tsiranana—president of independent Madagascar (1959–72)
Didier Ratsiraka—president of Madagascar's Second Republic (1975–93; 1997–2002)
Marc Ravalomanana—president of Madagascar (2002–present)
Charles Rabemananjara—prime minister of Madagascar (2007–present)

TIME LINE

IN MADAGASCAR	IN THE WORLD

1 A.D.
Madagascar is settled by Malayo-Polynesians.

1500
The Portuguese discover Madagascar, naming it the Isle of Saint Lawrence.

1650s
The kingdom of Sakalava on the western coast emerges.

1716
The Betsimisaraka empire emerges under Ratsimilaho, the son of an English pirate and a Malagasy princess.

1810–28
Reign of Radama I, a Merina king. He establishes the largest kingdom yet in Madagascar. British missionaries convert the court to Christianity. The British devise a Latin alphabet for the Merina dialect of Malagasy and set up a printing press. Merina culture begins to spread.

1828–61
Reign of Radama's successor

1861–63
Reign of Radama II

1883–85
The Franco-Malagasy War results in Madagascar's signing a peace treaty giving France greater influence in Malagasy affairs.

1896
France annexes Madagascar and unifies it under a single administration with Joseph Galliéni as governor-general.

1897
The Merina queen is exiled, and Madagascar is turned into a French protectorate.

1946
Madagascar becomes an Overseas Territory of France.

1947
A Merina insurrection for political rights is crushed by the French Army. As many as 80,000 Malagasy are killed.

1000 A.D.

1100
Rise of the Incan Civilization in Peru

1558–1603
Reign of Elizabeth I of England

1776
U.S. Declaration of Independence

1789–99
The French Revolution

1939
World War II begins.

1945
The United States drops atomic bombs on Hiroshima and Nagasaki.

IN MADAGASCAR	IN THE WORLD
1958 Madagascar votes for autonomy.	
1960 Madagascar gains independence on June 26. Philibert Tsiranana is elected as the first president of the Malagasy Republic.	**1966–69** The Chinese Cultural Revolution
1972 Tsiranana dissolves parliament amid popular unrest and hands power to General Gabriel Ramanantsoa.	
1975 Admiral Didier Ratsiraka stages a coup and changes the name of the country from the Malagasy Republic to the Democratic Republic of Madagascar.	**1986** Nuclear power disaster at Chernobyl in Ukraine
	1991 Breakup of the Soviet Union
1992 Ratsiraka introduces democratic reforms under public pressure, but is forced to resign.	
1993–96 Albert Zafy is elected president but is later found guilty of corruption and impeached.	
1997 Ratsiraka is voted back into office and restores some of his dictatorial powers.	**1997** Hong Kong is returned to China.
2001 The presidential election is held and Marc Ravalomanana claims outright victory.	**2003** War in Iraq begins.
2004 Tropical cyclones Elita and Gafilo hit Madagascar, leaving thousands homeless.	
2006 Ravalomanana is elected to his second term in office.	
2007 A revision to the constitution becomes effective in April. Some changes include redistricting the six autonomous provinces into 22 smaller regions, the expansion of presidential powers, and making English the third official language, after Malagasy and French.	

GLOSSARY

Alahamady Be
First new moon in first month of the Malagasy New Year.

aloalo (**a-LOOL**)
Carved memorial posts.

côtiers (**COH-ti-ay**)
Coastal people.

Eid ul Fitr (also Eid al-Fitr)
Muslim celebration to mark the end of Ramadan, a month of obligatory fasting.

fady (**FAH-di**)
Forbidden, taboo.

fanorona (**fan-or-OON**)
Malagasy board game.

faritra (**FAR-trr**)
Regions.

fokontany (**FOOK-on-TAN**)
Localized community rule.

haiteny (**HAY-ten-i**)
Traditional style of love poetry.

khat (**KAT**)
The leaves of this plant are chewed as a stimulant.

mofo (**MOOF**)
Malagasy bread.

mofo gasy (**MOOF gash**)
Malagasy bread made from a batter of sweetened rice flour.

ombiasy (**om-bi-ASH**)
Traditional healer.

paella
Seasoned rice with shrimp and chicken.

parique (**pa-REEK**)
Snack made from peanuts, rice, and sugar.

pousse-pousse (**POOSS-POOSS**)
Cart for passengers or goods, pulled by a man.

ranovola (**RAHN-o-VOOL**)
Water boiled with the crusty residue in the rice pot.

rougaille (**roo-GUY**)
Sauce made from tomatoes, ginger, onions, lemons, and hot peppers.

sodina (**so-DEEN**)
Traditional Malagasy flute.

tsingy (**TSING-i**)
Sharp limestone pinnacles.

valiha (**va-LEE-a**)
Musical instrument resembling a zither.

vintana (**vin-TARN**)
Person's fortune, fate, destiny.

FURTHER INFORMATION

BOOKS

Bishop, Nic. *Digging for Bird Dinosaurs: An Expedition to Madagascar.* Boston: Houghton Mifflin, 2000.

Bradt, Hilary, Derek Shuurman, and Nick Garbutt. *Madagascar Wildlife: A Visitor's Guide,* 2nd Edition. Gerrards Cross, England: Bradt Publications, 2001.

Corwin, Jeff, and Elaine Pascoe. *Into Wild Madagascar. The Jeff Corwin Experience.* San Diego, CA: Blackbirch Press, 2004.

Eveleigh, Mark. *Maverick in Madagascar.* London: Lonely Planet, 2001.

Kabana, Joni. *Torina's World: A Child's Life in Madagascar.* Portland, OR: Arnica Publishing, 2007.

Oluonye, Mary N. *Madagascar.* Minneapolis, MN: Carolrhoda Books, 2000.

Pakenham, Thomas. *The Remarkable Baobab.* London: Weidenfeld & Nicolson, 2004.

Tyson, Peter. *The Eighth Continent: Life, Death, and Discovery in the Lost World of Madagascar.* New York: Perennial, 2001.

WEB SITES

8th Continent: Travels Through Madagascar. www.8thcontinent.nl

BBC News Country Profile: Madagascar. http://news.bbc.co.uk/1/hi/world/africa/country_profiles/1063208.stm

Central Intelligence Agency World Factbook (Click World Factbook, then select Madagascar from country list). www.cia.gov/index.html

Greatest Places: Madagascar. www.greatestplaces.org/book_pages/madagascar2.htm

The Living Edens: A World Apart. www.pbs.org/edens/madagascar

Lonely Planet World Guide: Madagascar. www.lonelyplanet.com/worldguide/destinations/africa/madagascar

Madagascar. www.wildmadagascar.org

Report on Madagascar: A Thousand Hills & Thousands of Wills. www.winne.com/madagascar/madagascar.html

Visit Madagascar: www.visitmadagascar.com

FILMS

Madagascar. Activision/Dreamworks, 2005.

Quand les Étoiles Rencontrent la Mer (*When the Stars Meet the Sea*). Jacques Le Glou. Audiovisuel/La Sept Cinema/Canal Horizons, 1996.

MUSIC

The Music of Madagascar: Classic Traditional Recordings of the 1930s. Various artists. Yazoo, 1995.

Rough Guide to the Music of Madagascar. Various artists. World Music Network, 2005.

BIBLIOGRAPHY

Bradt, Hilary. *Guide to Madagascar.* Guilford, CT: Globe Pequot Press; Bucks, UK: Bradt Publications, 1994.

———. *Madagascar: The Bradt Travel Guide,* 8th Edition. Guilford, CT: Globe Pequot Press; Bucks, UK: Bradt Publications, 2005.

Fitzpatrick, Mary and Paul Greenway. *Madagascar.* Victoria, Australia: Lonely Planet, 2001.

Lerner Editors. *Madagascar—In Pictures.* Minneapolis, MN: Lerner Publications, 1988.

Morris, Neil. *The World's Top Ten Islands.* London: Belitha Press. 1995.

Swaney, Deanna and Robert Willcox. *Madagascar & Comoros.* Victoria, Australia: Lonely Planet, 1994.

Encyclopedia of the Nations: Madagascar. www.nationsencyclopedia.com/Africa/Madagascar.html

Library of Congress: A Country Study: Madagascar. http://lcweb2.loc.gov/frd/cs/mgtoc.html

Madagascar—Encyclopaedia Britannica. www.britannica.com/eb/article-9108476/Madagascar

Madagascar—Environmental Profile. http://rainforests.mongabay.com/20madagascar.htm

INDEX